All About Suez Canal: A Kid's Guide to the World's Most Important Waterway

Educational Books For Kids, Volume 13

Shah Rukh

Published by Shah Rukh, 2024.

While every precaution has been taken in the preparation of this book, the publisher assumes no responsibility for errors or omissions, or for damages resulting from the use of the information contained herein.

ALL ABOUT SUEZ CANAL: A KID'S GUIDE TO THE WORLD'S MOST IMPORTANT WATERWAY

First edition. September 22, 2024.

Copyright © 2024 Shah Rukh.

ISBN: 979-8227163431

Written by Shah Rukh.

Table of Contents

Prologue

Welcome to *All About Suez Canal: A Kid's Guide to the World's Most Important Waterway*! Imagine a place where ships from all over the world sail through a narrow channel, connecting two vast oceans and saving weeks of travel time. This incredible place is the Suez Canal, one of the most important waterways on our planet.

But the Suez Canal is more than just a shortcut for ships. It's a story of dreams, determination, and global impact. From the first ideas of connecting the Mediterranean Sea to the Red Sea thousands of years ago to the modern engineering marvel it is today, the Suez Canal has played a crucial role in shaping our world. Wars have been fought over it, empires have risen and fallen, and countless goods and treasures have passed through its waters.

In this book, you'll embark on a journey through time, learning about the incredible history, the people who made it possible, and the ships that sailed through it. You'll discover how this narrow strip of water has influenced everything from global trade to the environment and what the future holds for this vital waterway.

Whether you're a curious explorer or a young historian, this book will help you dive deep into the fascinating world of the Suez Canal. So, let's set sail and explore the wonders of one of the most remarkable places on Earth!

Chapter 1: The Dream of Connecting Seas

The idea of connecting seas has been a dream for centuries, a vision that captivated explorers, rulers, and traders alike. This dream of creating a waterway that would link two major bodies of water—the Mediterranean Sea and the Red Sea—stirred the imagination of ancient civilizations long before the construction of the Suez Canal became a reality. The motivation behind this dream was clear: to facilitate faster, more efficient trade routes. Instead of sailing around the southern tip of Africa, a long and dangerous journey, ships could pass directly from Europe to Asia through a man-made waterway. This would not only save time and resources but also open up new economic opportunities, bringing prosperity to those who controlled the passage.

The ancient Egyptians were among the first to imagine such a connection. As early as 2000 BCE, Pharaoh Senusret III is said to have explored the possibility of connecting the Red Sea to the Nile River, which would eventually lead to the Mediterranean Sea. However, the challenges were immense. The technology of the time made it difficult to envision a massive construction project like the one we know today. Moreover, maintaining a canal that could withstand the changing landscape, desert sands, and the different water levels of the two seas seemed impossible. Despite these obstacles, the idea never fully disappeared, and it was revisited by different leaders and civilizations throughout history.

The Persians, under the reign of Darius the Great around 500 BCE, took the dream a step further by attempting to create a canal that would connect the Nile to the Red Sea. Darius, understanding the strategic and economic importance of such a route, saw it as a way to strengthen his empire's influence over trade between Europe and Asia. His engineers managed to dig a canal that allowed small ships to pass through, but it was far from the grand vision that would later be realized with the Suez Canal. The canal created by Darius eventually fell into disuse, yet the dream of a permanent link between the two seas remained alive.

Centuries later, the dream would resurface during the time of the Romans, who also recognized the potential of such a canal. Emperor Trajan considered building a waterway to connect the Mediterranean and Red Seas, but like those before him, the task proved to be too monumental given the technology and resources available at the time. While no significant progress was made during this period, the idea continued to linger in the minds of rulers and visionaries, passing from one generation to the next.

Fast forward to the Middle Ages, and the dream had not faded. The Islamic Caliphate, under the rule of Caliph Al-Mansur in the 8th century, explored the possibility of reopening the ancient canal that Darius had constructed. However, like many attempts before, the project was abandoned, this time due to military and political concerns. Still, the concept of connecting seas persisted, as rulers and merchants understood the profound impact it could have on the movement of goods and people.

It wasn't until the modern era that this age-old dream started to become a tangible reality. In the 19th century, the vision of connecting the Mediterranean and Red Seas gained new momentum, this time driven by advances in engineering and a new wave of global trade. The rise of European powers, particularly France and Britain, intensified the desire for faster trade routes to their colonies in Asia and Africa. The dream of connecting the seas was no longer just a theoretical ambition but a necessity for maintaining global dominance and economic strength.

One of the key figures in bringing this dream closer to realization was Ferdinand de Lesseps, a French diplomat and engineer. De Lesseps became fascinated by the idea of constructing a canal through the

Isthmus of Suez, a narrow strip of land separating the two seas. He believed that with modern engineering techniques, the centuries-old dream could finally come true. De Lesseps managed to gather support from various governments and investors, convincing them of the canal's potential benefits. His vision was not just about connecting two seas, but about transforming global trade and shortening the distance between Europe and Asia by thousands of miles.

The construction of the Suez Canal, however, was not without its challenges. The land itself was unforgiving, with vast deserts and shifting sands complicating the project. The workforce, composed largely of Egyptian laborers, faced grueling conditions as they dug through the harsh terrain. There were also political obstacles, as various nations sought to control the project for their own interests. Despite these difficulties, the dream pressed forward, driven by the determination of those who understood its monumental significance.

Finally, in 1869, the Suez Canal was completed, marking the realization of a dream that had persisted for thousands of years. Ships could now pass directly between the Mediterranean and Red Seas, revolutionizing global trade in ways that had only been imagined by ancient civilizations. The dream of connecting seas had not only come true but had surpassed all expectations in its impact on the world. The canal became a vital artery for international trade, allowing ships to avoid the long, perilous journey around Africa's Cape of Good Hope.

The significance of the Suez Canal extends far beyond its physical construction. It represents the culmination of centuries of human ambition, determination, and ingenuity. The canal's creation brought new wealth and power to the nations that controlled it, while also opening up opportunities for economic growth across the globe. It became a symbol of humanity's ability to shape the world to its will, overcoming natural barriers and turning dreams into reality. The long-held aspiration of connecting the Mediterranean and Red Seas finally materialized into a waterway that would forever change the course of history.

This dream, which had captured the imaginations of pharaohs, emperors, and caliphs alike, is now a vital part of the global economy, proving that sometimes the most ambitious dreams are worth pursuing, no matter how long they take to come true. Today, the Suez Canal stands as a testament to the power of human vision and persistence, a reminder that the dreams of connecting seas were not only about improving trade but about bridging continents and bringing the world closer together.

Chapter 2: The Birth of the Suez Canal

The birth of the Suez Canal is one of the most remarkable feats of human engineering, a project that transformed global trade and reshaped the political and economic landscape of the world. Its story begins long before construction started, stretching back to ancient times when rulers, explorers, and traders dreamt of connecting the Mediterranean Sea and the Red Sea through a man-made passage. This desire for a direct route between Europe and Asia was driven by the immense potential for faster and safer trade, allowing ships to bypass the long and treacherous voyage around the southern tip of Africa. However, despite centuries of attempts and aspirations, the realization of this dream did not come until the 19th century, when modern technology and geopolitical factors aligned to make the Suez Canal a reality.

By the early 1800s, Europe was entering an era of rapid industrialization and colonial expansion. The demand for efficient trade routes grew as European powers sought to establish and maintain their empires in Africa and Asia. This was especially true for Britain and France, which had significant colonies in India and Southeast Asia. The journey from Europe to these regions required navigating the Cape of Good Hope at the southern tip of Africa, a long and dangerous route that added months to voyages and involved significant risks, from unpredictable weather to pirates. The need for a quicker and more direct route became increasingly urgent.

During the reign of Muhammad Ali, the ruler of Egypt in the early 19th century, discussions about constructing a canal across the Isthmus of Suez started to gain traction. Although he focused more on modernizing Egypt's infrastructure and military, Muhammad Ali recognized the strategic importance of controlling such a canal and explored the possibility of its construction. However, it was not until the mid-19th century that serious efforts began to turn this long-standing idea into a practical project.

Ferdinand de Lesseps, a French diplomat and engineer, emerged as the visionary who would bring the Suez Canal into existence. De Lesseps had served as the French consul in Egypt, where he developed close relationships with Egyptian officials and became convinced that a canal linking the Mediterranean and Red Seas was not only feasible but essential for global trade. After years of lobbying for support, de Lesseps secured permission from the Egyptian ruler, Sa'id Pasha, to begin the project. In 1854, de Lesseps founded the Suez Canal Company, an international enterprise designed to finance, build, and operate the canal. This marked the beginning of a new chapter in the history of global trade, one that would change the world forever.

The construction of the Suez Canal was no small feat. The Isthmus of Suez, a narrow strip of land separating the Mediterranean from the Red Sea, was a harsh, unforgiving landscape. Workers had to contend with extreme heat, sandstorms, and shifting desert sands that made the work both dangerous and physically exhausting. The labor force consisted largely of Egyptian workers, many of whom were forced into service through a system of corvée labor, a practice that required peasants to work on government projects for no pay. These laborers, numbering in the tens of thousands, faced brutal conditions, working long hours in the desert sun with little access to food, water, or medical care. Many fell victim to disease, malnutrition, and exhaustion, and the human cost of the canal's construction was staggering.

Despite these hardships, the project moved forward, thanks to de Lesseps' determination and the expertise of engineers who utilized the latest technology of the time. Steam-powered dredgers were employed to dig through the sandy terrain, and new surveying techniques were used to ensure that the canal's course would remain stable. One of the most challenging aspects of the project was ensuring that the canal could accommodate ships of all sizes, from small trading vessels to the massive steamships that were becoming more common in global trade. To do this, the canal needed to be deep and wide enough to allow for safe passage, a task that required precision and meticulous planning.

The geopolitical implications of the Suez Canal were immense. For European powers, especially Britain and France, the canal represented a crucial strategic asset. Whoever controlled the canal would control the primary trade route between Europe and Asia, giving them a significant advantage in global commerce and military power. This became evident as the project progressed, with both Britain and France competing for influence over the canal and the region. Britain, in particular, was concerned about maintaining access to its colonies in India and the Far East, and British officials kept a close eye on the canal's development.

As construction neared completion, the world began to recognize the significance of what was happening in Egypt. The canal was more than just a waterway; it was a symbol of the new era of globalization, a time when the world was becoming more connected through advances in technology and transportation. For Egypt, the canal was seen as a potential source of immense wealth and power, as it would place the country at the crossroads of global trade. However, this potential was not without its risks. The financial cost of the canal was enormous, and Egypt had taken on significant debt to fund its construction, a burden that would have lasting consequences.

After ten years of labor, setbacks, and challenges, the Suez Canal was finally completed in 1869. On November 17 of that year, an elaborate ceremony marked the opening of the canal to the world. Dignitaries from across Europe and the Middle East gathered to witness the first ships pass through the canal, a historic moment that signaled the beginning of a new era in global trade. The canal, stretching over 100 miles from Port Said on the Mediterranean coast to Suez on the Red Sea, instantly became one of the most important waterways in the world.

The opening of the Suez Canal had a profound impact on global trade. Ships could now travel between Europe and Asia in a fraction of the time it had previously taken, dramatically reducing shipping costs and opening up new markets for goods and resources. The canal became a lifeline for European empires, particularly Britain, which relied on it to maintain its hold over India and other colonies. The "lifeline of the empire," as it was called, allowed Britain to transport troops, supplies, and goods quickly and efficiently, solidifying its dominance in the region.

However, the financial burden of the canal, combined with poor economic management, led Egypt into a debt crisis. By the 1870s, Egypt was struggling to repay its loans, and its economy was in shambles. In an effort to stave off bankruptcy, the Egyptian government was forced to sell its shares in the Suez Canal Company to Britain in 1875. This move gave Britain control over the canal and marked the beginning of British dominance in Egypt, a situation that would persist until the mid-20th century.

For the next several decades, the Suez Canal would play a central role in global trade and geopolitics. It became a flashpoint in international relations, with various powers vying for control over this strategic waterway. During World War I and World War II, the canal was a vital military asset, allowing Allied forces to move troops and supplies between Europe and Asia. Control of the canal was fiercely contested, and its strategic importance only grew as the world became more interconnected.

In 1956, the canal would once again become the center of global attention during the Suez Crisis. Egyptian President Gamal Abdel Nasser, seeking to assert Egypt's independence from Western influence, nationalized the canal, seizing control from Britain and France. This move sparked an international crisis, with Britain, France, and Israel launching a military intervention to retake the canal. The crisis ultimately ended with a diplomatic resolution brokered by the United Nations, and Egypt retained control of the canal.

Today, the Suez Canal remains one of the most important waterways in the world, handling roughly 12% of global trade. It continues to be a symbol of the triumph of human ingenuity, a testament to the vision of those who dreamed of connecting seas and transforming global commerce. The birth of the Suez Canal, with all its challenges, triumphs, and political complexities, stands as one of the defining moments in modern history, shaping the course of trade, industry, and international relations for generations to come.

Chapter 3: Building the Great Waterway

Building the Suez Canal, often referred to as the "Great Waterway," was an extraordinary achievement that stands as one of the most ambitious construction projects in history. This colossal endeavor, which took over a decade to complete, required immense planning, coordination, and determination. The canal was envisioned as a shortcut between Europe and Asia, bypassing the need to sail around the southern tip of Africa, thus dramatically reducing travel time for ships engaged in global trade. The realization of this vision was the result of both technological advancements and the willpower of key individuals who refused to let the obstacles they faced deter them from achieving their goal.

The process of building the canal began with immense political and financial negotiations. In the mid-19th century, Egypt was under the control of the Ottoman Empire, but it was ruled by a local leader, Khedive Sa'id Pasha, who was keen on modernizing the country. French diplomat and engineer Ferdinand de Lesseps played a pivotal role in convincing Sa'id Pasha of the benefits of constructing a canal across the Isthmus of Suez. De Lesseps was a charismatic and determined figure, who had served as a diplomat in Egypt and developed a close relationship with the Egyptian ruler. He believed that the time had come to turn the centuries-old dream of connecting the Mediterranean and Red Seas into reality.

In 1854, de Lesseps secured a concession from Sa'id Pasha to form a company that would oversee the construction and operation of the canal. This was the beginning of the Suez Canal Company, an international venture that would finance, build, and manage the waterway. With the concession in hand, de Lesseps began the challenging task of gathering support and funding from investors, particularly in Europe. The political and financial backing of France was critical, as the project required a vast amount of capital to cover the costs of construction, labor, and infrastructure. The British government, however, remained skeptical, as they were concerned about the potential for French influence in the region and the strategic implications of the canal for their trade routes to India.

Once the financial and political foundations were laid, the actual construction of the canal began in earnest in 1859. The task at hand was monumental, and the engineering challenges were unlike anything attempted before. The canal would need to stretch over 100 miles from Port Said on the Mediterranean Sea to Suez on the Red Sea, cutting through the desert landscape of the Isthmus of Suez. The terrain itself presented significant difficulties, as the region was largely composed of desert sands, with no natural water sources along the proposed route. Furthermore, the Mediterranean Sea and the Red Sea were at different elevations, which meant that precise calculations were needed to ensure that the canal could accommodate the flow of water and allow ships to pass through without obstruction.

To overcome these challenges, de Lesseps and his team of engineers turned to the latest advancements in construction technology. One of the key innovations used in the construction of the Suez Canal was the steam-powered dredger, a machine that could dig through the sand and soil more efficiently than manual labor alone. These dredgers were vital for removing the vast amounts of earth needed to create a channel deep and wide enough to allow ships to pass through. However, steam-powered machines were still relatively new at the time, and the project was one of the first large-scale uses of such technology in civil engineering.

Despite the use of advanced machinery, the construction of the canal still relied heavily on manual labor. Tens of thousands of Egyptian workers, many of whom were forced into service through a system of corvée labor, toiled under harsh and grueling conditions to dig the canal. These laborers were tasked with digging, carrying earth, and clearing the land for the passage of ships, often working long hours in the scorching desert heat. The work was physically exhausting, and the conditions were brutal, with little access to clean water, food, or medical care. As a result, many laborers succumbed to disease, malnutrition, and exhaustion. The human cost of building the Suez Canal was enormous, with estimates suggesting that tens of thousands of workers lost their lives during the construction process.

In addition to the physical challenges of the terrain and the harsh conditions for workers, the construction of the canal faced political and logistical obstacles as well. International tensions surrounding the project were high, particularly between France and Britain. While the French were heavily involved in the project, British interests in the region grew as the strategic importance of the canal became more apparent. The British were particularly concerned about maintaining access to their colonies in India, and they feared that French control of the canal would threaten their dominance in global trade. This led to a complex political balancing act, as both powers sought to secure influence over the project without causing open conflict.

The construction process was marked by several major engineering challenges, including the problem of connecting the canal to natural water sources. Unlike other canals, such as the Panama Canal, the Suez Canal does not rely on locks to manage changes in elevation. Instead, the canal is a "sea-level" canal, meaning that the water flows naturally between the Mediterranean and Red Seas. However, this presented its own set of difficulties, as the engineers had to ensure that the water levels would remain consistent throughout the canal's length, despite differences in tidal patterns between the two seas. To address this issue, the engineers constructed a series of basins and reservoirs along the canal's route, which helped regulate the flow of water and maintain the necessary depth for ships to pass through.

As the construction progressed, it became clear that the project would take longer and cost more than initially anticipated. The harsh desert conditions, combined with the immense scale of the project, led to frequent delays and budget overruns. Despite these setbacks, de Lesseps remained committed to the project, tirelessly working to secure additional funding and resources to keep construction on track. His determination, along with the expertise of the engineers and workers involved, eventually paid off.

After ten years of relentless labor, the Suez Canal was completed in 1869. The grand opening of the canal was a momentous occasion, celebrated with a lavish ceremony attended by dignitaries from across Europe and the Middle East. Empress Eugenie of France, wife of Emperor Napoleon III, presided over the opening festivities, symbolizing France's central role in the project. The first ships passed through the canal, marking the culmination of years of planning, hard work, and determination.

The completion of the Suez Canal was more than just a technological triumph; it was a transformative event in global trade and politics. The canal instantly became one of the most important shipping routes in the world, allowing ships to travel between Europe and Asia in a fraction of the time it had previously taken. The canal reduced the need for ships to navigate around the Cape of Good Hope at the southern tip of Africa, cutting thousands of miles and several weeks off the journey. This had a profound impact on global trade, as goods could now be transported more quickly and efficiently between Europe, Asia, and Africa.

The strategic importance of the canal also became apparent almost immediately. For European powers, particularly Britain, the canal was a vital lifeline for maintaining control over their colonies in India and other parts of Asia. The British government, initially skeptical of the project, quickly realized the canal's significance and moved to secure its interests in the region. In 1875, just a few years after the canal's completion, the British government purchased a controlling stake in the Suez Canal Company, giving Britain significant influence over the operation of the canal. This move was driven by British Prime Minister

Benjamin Disraeli, who recognized the canal's value as a strategic asset for the British Empire.

Over the following decades, the Suez Canal became an indispensable part of global shipping and a symbol of the growing interconnectedness of the world. Its construction opened up new markets and opportunities for trade, facilitating the exchange of goods, people, and ideas across continents. The canal also became a focal point of geopolitical tensions, with various powers vying for control over this crucial waterway. The importance of the canal only increased with the advent of modern steamships and the expansion of global empires.

The construction of the Suez Canal was not only a defining moment in the history of engineering and trade but also a testament to the vision and perseverance of those who believed in its potential. Despite the immense challenges, both technological and political, the canal was successfully completed and has remained a critical artery for global commerce for over 150 years. Today, the Suez Canal continues to play a central role in the global economy, handling a significant portion of the world's shipping traffic and serving as a reminder of the power of human ingenuity to reshape the world.

The birth of this great waterway was a turning point in history, a project that required unprecedented coordination and effort. It forever changed the landscape of global trade, making the world more connected and bringing distant regions closer together in ways that were previously unimaginable. The Suez Canal stands not only as a remarkable engineering achievement but also as a symbol of the aspirations and dreams of those who sought to bridge the gap between continents, turning a once-impossible vision into a lasting reality.

Chapter 4: The First Ships Through the Canal

The passage of the first ships through the newly completed Suez Canal in 1869 was a momentous occasion, an event that captured the imagination of the world and marked the dawn of a new era in global trade and transportation. This monumental milestone came after over a decade of immense labor, political maneuvering, and innovative engineering. The spectacle of the first ships traversing the canal symbolized not only the success of the ambitious project but also the ushering in of a new chapter in history, where continents were more interconnected than ever before, and the distances that separated them could now be bridged with unprecedented ease.

The ceremony marking the official opening of the Suez Canal was an international affair, attended by dignitaries, heads of state, and royalty from across Europe and the Middle East. It was a reflection of the global significance of the canal and its promise to revolutionize trade routes between the East and West. Among the most notable figures present was Empress Eugénie of France, the wife of Emperor Napoleon III, whose nation had played a key role in the construction and financing of the canal. Her presence underscored the French pride in what was seen as a grand engineering triumph that would forever be associated with the name of its French architect, Ferdinand de Lesseps.

On November 17, 1869, the first ships officially sailed through the canal, marking the culmination of years of effort and perseverance. The canal's inaugural passage was led by the French imperial yacht, L'Aigle, which carried Empress Eugénie as the guest of honor. L'Aigle was followed by a flotilla of ships from various countries, forming a grand procession that made its way from the Mediterranean to the Red Sea. These ships, representing the global powers of the time, carried diplomats, investors, engineers, and journalists, all eager to witness the historic event that promised to reshape the world's maritime landscape.

The journey of the first ships through the Suez Canal was no ordinary voyage. It was a carefully choreographed event designed to showcase the technological marvel of the canal and demonstrate the ease with which ships could now move between Europe and Asia. The passage began at Port Said, a bustling harbor on the northern entrance of the canal, where the Mediterranean Sea met the isthmus. From there, the ships would travel southward along the canal's 100-mile stretch, passing through a series of lakes and basins before reaching the Red Sea at the southern terminus of Suez.

The procession of ships was greeted by crowds of onlookers who had gathered along the canal's banks to witness the historic moment. The air was filled with excitement and celebration as cannons fired salutes and flags from different nations fluttered in the breeze. The first ships to pass through the canal were adorned with colorful banners, symbolizing the unity of nations in this shared achievement. This was a time when the world was becoming increasingly interconnected, and the Suez Canal was a symbol of that growing interconnectedness.

The journey of the first ships through the canal was not only a ceremonial event but also a test of the canal's capabilities. The engineers who had worked tirelessly to design and build the canal were eager to see how it would perform under real-world conditions. Would the canal's depth and width be sufficient to accommodate large ships? Would the water flow smoothly between the two seas? These were questions that needed to be answered, and the passage of the first ships would provide the answers.

As the ships made their way down the canal, they encountered a series of artificial lakes that had been constructed along the route to regulate the water level and provide resting points for ships traveling through the canal. One of the largest of these lakes was Lake Timsah, located roughly halfway along the canal's length. This lake served as a critical reservoir, helping to maintain the water level in the canal and ensuring that the ships could pass through without obstruction. The presence of these lakes was a key feature of the Suez Canal's design, setting it apart from other canals that relied on locks to manage changes in elevation.

As the first ships moved through the narrow channel, they encountered the canal's most striking feature: its sea-level design. Unlike other major canals, such as the Panama Canal, the Suez Canal did not require a system of locks to raise or lower ships between different elevations. Instead, the engineers had constructed the canal at sea level, allowing ships to move seamlessly from one sea to the other. This innovation was made possible by the relatively flat terrain of the Suez Isthmus and the careful planning of the engineers who ensured that the water levels would remain consistent throughout the canal's length.

While the passage of the first ships through the canal was largely smooth, there were moments of tension and uncertainty. Some ships found it difficult to navigate the narrow sections of the canal, particularly those with larger hulls. In these instances, the pilots relied on the canal's dredgers and support boats to guide the ships through the tight spaces. These challenges were a reminder that, while the canal was a remarkable achievement, it would require ongoing maintenance and adjustments to accommodate the growing size and volume of global shipping.

As the flotilla of ships approached the southern end of the canal, the anticipation among the passengers and crew grew. The sight of the Red Sea on the horizon was a powerful symbol of the canal's success. For centuries, traders and explorers had dreamed of a direct route between Europe and Asia, and now that dream had become a reality. The ships passed through the final section of the canal and emerged into the open waters of the Red Sea, completing their journey from the Mediterranean. The moment was met with jubilation and celebration, as the first ships to pass through the Suez Canal had proven that the great waterway was not only feasible but a resounding success.

The completion of the first passage through the Suez Canal had far-reaching implications for global trade and geopolitics. The canal instantly became one of the most important shipping routes in the world, dramatically reducing the time and cost of transporting goods between Europe, Asia, and Africa. Before the canal's construction, ships traveling between Europe and Asia had to make the long and treacherous journey around the southern tip of Africa, navigating the dangerous waters of the Cape of Good Hope. With the opening of the Suez Canal, that journey was shortened by thousands of miles and several weeks, providing a faster, safer, and more efficient route for global commerce.

The economic impact of the canal was felt almost immediately. European powers, particularly Britain and France, saw the canal as a vital lifeline for their colonies and trade routes. For the British, the canal was especially important, as it provided a direct route to India, one of the crown jewels of the British Empire. The canal allowed British ships to transport goods, troops, and resources between Europe and India more quickly and efficiently than ever before. As a result, the British government became increasingly interested in securing control over the canal, and in 1875, just a few years after its opening, Britain purchased a controlling stake in the Suez Canal Company.

The strategic importance of the canal also made it a focal point of international diplomacy and conflict. Control over the canal became a critical issue for the world's major powers, and its location at the crossroads of Europe, Asia, and Africa made it a key asset in global geopolitics. Over the years, the canal would become the site of several military conflicts, including the Suez Crisis of 1956, when Egypt nationalized the canal, sparking an international confrontation with Britain, France, and Israel.

Beyond its economic and political significance, the passage of the first ships through the Suez Canal also had a profound cultural impact. The canal was seen as a symbol of human ingenuity and progress, a testament to what could be achieved through determination, cooperation, and innovation. It was a marvel of engineering, a feat that had been dreamed of for centuries but only became possible through the combined efforts of visionaries like Ferdinand de Lesseps, the engineers who designed the canal, and the tens of thousands of laborers who toiled to bring it to life.

The first ships to pass through the canal represented more than just a new trade route; they were a symbol of the interconnectedness of the world and the possibilities of the modern era. The Suez Canal stood as a bridge between East and West, a gateway that brought distant cultures and economies closer together. It was a triumph of human ambition, one that reshaped the global economy and forever changed the way goods, people, and ideas moved across the world.

In the years that followed the passage of the first ships, the Suez Canal became an indispensable part of the global shipping network. Its importance only grew with the rise of modern industrial economies, as the demand for faster and more efficient transportation of goods increased. The canal facilitated the movement of oil, textiles, spices, and countless other commodities, fueling the growth of global trade and contributing to the economic development of nations around the world. Today, the Suez Canal remains a vital artery of global commerce, handling a significant portion of the world's shipping traffic and continuing to play a central role in the global economy.

The journey of those first ships through the Suez Canal was a moment that would be remembered for generations. It was the culmination of centuries of dreaming, decades of planning, and years of hard work. The canal transformed the world's maritime landscape, bringing nations closer together and opening up new opportunities for trade and cooperation. The passage of the first ships was not just the beginning of a new era in global trade—it was a symbol of human progress, a reminder of what could be achieved when people came together to pursue a common vision.

Chapter 5: The Canal's Role in World Trade

The Suez Canal has been one of the most pivotal waterways in shaping the course of global trade since its completion in 1869. Its role in world trade is nothing short of revolutionary, as it altered not only the physical routes that connected continents but also the economic, political, and social dynamics of nations and empires. At its core, the Suez Canal offers a critical shortcut for ships traveling between Europe and Asia, significantly reducing the time and distance required to transport goods across these vast and strategically vital regions. By allowing vessels to bypass the treacherous journey around the southern tip of Africa, the canal opened up new possibilities for trade, making the movement of goods faster, cheaper, and safer than ever before. The impact of the canal has only grown since its inception, as it continues to serve as one of the most important arteries in the global economy.

Before the Suez Canal, ships traveling between Europe and Asia had to navigate around the Cape of Good Hope at the southern tip of Africa, a route that added thousands of miles and several weeks to their journeys. This long, perilous voyage exposed ships to dangerous weather conditions and hostile waters, and the added time and expense of the journey made it less profitable for traders to engage in large-scale commerce between Europe, Asia, and Africa. The completion of the Suez Canal changed all of that. By connecting the Mediterranean Sea to the Red Sea, the canal created a direct and navigable route between Europe and Asia. This meant that instead of traveling around Africa, ships could now cut through the canal, reducing the voyage by over 4,000 miles and saving an average of 10 to 15 days of travel time. The canal, in essence, served as a bridge that brought continents closer together, making international trade far more efficient.

The economic implications of this development were immediate and profound. The Suez Canal became a vital lifeline for global trade, facilitating the rapid transport of goods such as textiles, spices, tea, and raw materials between Europe and Asia. For countries like Britain, which was heavily invested in colonial holdings such as India, the canal provided a critical link to its overseas territories. The canal allowed British merchants to export goods from Britain to India and import Indian products back to Europe more swiftly and profitably than ever before. The same applied to other European powers with colonies and interests in Asia, including France and the Netherlands. These colonial empires depended on fast and reliable access to their territories in Asia, and the Suez Canal provided just that. It reduced the costs of shipping and made it possible for more frequent voyages, thus bolstering trade between Europe and the East.

Beyond the immediate trade benefits, the Suez Canal played a significant role in shaping global geopolitics. Control over the canal was seen as essential for maintaining dominance in world trade, and nations vied for influence over this strategic waterway. For example, Britain recognized the strategic importance of the canal for maintaining its trade routes to India, and in 1875, it bought a controlling stake in the Suez Canal Company from the financially struggling Khedive of Egypt. This gave Britain significant control over the canal, and by extension, a dominant position in the global economy. The acquisition of the canal ensured that Britain could safeguard its trade routes and maintain its dominance as a global maritime power well into the 20th century. It also marked the beginning of a long period during which the canal became a flashpoint for international diplomacy and conflict, as different powers sought to control this critical artery of global commerce.

The impact of the Suez Canal on global trade was not limited to Europe and Asia. It also played a crucial role in connecting other parts of the world to these regions. For example, goods from Africa, the Middle East, and even the Americas could be transported through the canal to reach markets in Europe and Asia more efficiently. The canal acted as a global crossroads, facilitating trade between continents and helping to integrate the economies of distant regions. This interconnectedness was especially important during the Industrial Revolution, as the demand for raw materials and finished goods grew exponentially. European powers, with their vast industrial production capabilities, needed access to resources from around the world, and the Suez Canal made it easier to obtain these materials and transport them to the factories of Europe. Conversely, the canal allowed European countries to export their manufactured goods to markets in Asia and Africa, further boosting global trade.

As the 19th century gave way to the 20th, the Suez Canal's role in global trade only grew in importance. The canal became a vital passage for the transportation of oil, a commodity that would come to dominate world trade in the 20th century. As demand for oil increased with the rise of the automobile, aviation, and other industries, the Suez Canal provided a direct route for oil shipments from the Middle East to Europe and beyond. The Middle East, with its vast oil reserves, became a critical supplier of energy to the industrialized world, and the canal played a central role in ensuring that this supply could reach global markets. By transporting oil through the canal, producers in the Middle East could save time and costs, while consumers in Europe could access the energy they needed more quickly and affordably.

The canal's role in transporting oil became even more significant during times of global crisis, such as World War II. During the war, the Suez Canal was a crucial strategic asset for the Allied powers, as it allowed them to transport troops, supplies, and oil between the different theaters of war. The Axis powers recognized the importance of the canal and sought to disrupt Allied shipping by targeting the canal and the ships passing through it. Despite these efforts, the Allies managed to maintain control of the canal, ensuring that it remained open for the duration of the war. After the war, the canal continued to play a central role in global trade, as the world economy rebuilt itself and oil became even more important in powering the post-war economic boom.

In the latter half of the 20th century, the canal faced its most serious challenges during the Suez Crisis of 1956. By this time, Egypt had gained its independence, and President Gamal Abdel Nasser sought to assert Egyptian control over the canal by nationalizing it. This move was seen as a threat to Western interests, particularly those of Britain and France, who relied on the canal for their trade routes. In response, Britain, France, and Israel launched a military intervention to seize control of the canal. The crisis escalated into a major international incident, with the United States, the Soviet Union, and the United Nations all getting involved to broker a resolution. Ultimately, Nasser's nationalization of the canal was upheld, and Egypt gained control over the waterway, but the crisis highlighted the canal's importance in global trade and geopolitics.

Even after the Suez Crisis, the canal remained a critical artery for global commerce. However, the rise of container shipping and the increasing size of ships presented new challenges for the canal. In response, the Suez Canal Authority undertook several expansions and modernization projects to accommodate larger vessels and increase the canal's capacity. These efforts culminated in the opening of the Suez Canal Expansion Project in 2015, which added a new parallel channel to allow two-way traffic and reduce congestion. The expansion project increased the canal's capacity to handle the largest container ships in the world, ensuring that it would remain a vital part of global trade well into the 21st century.

Today, the Suez Canal continues to be one of the most important and busiest waterways in the world. It handles roughly 10% of global trade and around 12% of total seaborne trade, with thousands of ships passing through each year. The canal is particularly critical for the transportation of energy, as it serves as a major route for oil and liquefied natural gas (LNG) shipments from the Middle East to Europe and North America. In fact, the canal is so essential to the global energy supply that any disruption to its operations, even for a short period, can have significant impacts on oil prices and energy markets. This was evident in 2021 when the Ever Given, a massive container ship, became lodged in the canal, blocking traffic for several days and causing delays in global shipping. The incident underscored the canal's importance in the global supply chain and the fragility of the interconnected system that depends on its smooth operation.

In addition to its role in energy transportation, the canal is also a key route for the shipment of manufactured goods, agricultural products, and other commodities. The canal's strategic location at the crossroads of Europe, Asia, and Africa makes it an indispensable link in the global supply chain, facilitating the movement of goods between some of the world's largest and fastest-growing markets. For countries in the Asia-Pacific region, the Suez Canal provides a vital link to markets in Europe and the Middle East, while European countries rely on the canal to access raw materials and finished products from Asia and Africa.

The canal's importance in world trade is not just economic but also political. Control over the canal has been a source of tension and conflict for over a century, as different nations have sought to secure their interests in this strategically vital waterway. Even today, the canal remains a focal point of international diplomacy, as countries and companies alike recognize the importance of maintaining access to this critical trade route. In many ways, the Suez Canal serves as a microcosm of the global economy—an interconnected and interdependent system in which the actions of one country or company can have far-reaching consequences for the rest of the world.

Looking to the future, the Suez Canal is likely to remain a key player in world trade for years to come. As global trade continues to grow and evolve, the canal will play a central role in facilitating the movement of goods between continents and ensuring that the global supply chain remains efficient and reliable. While the canal faces challenges from competing routes, such as the Arctic shipping lanes, its strategic location and long history of success make it an indispensable part of the global trade network. The canal's continued expansion and modernization efforts will ensure that it remains relevant in a rapidly changing world, cementing its role as one of the most important waterways in the history of global commerce.

Chapter 6: Suez Canal and the Age of Steamships

The Suez Canal and the age of steamships are intricately linked in history, as both marked the dawn of a new era in global maritime trade, technology, and transportation. Together, they revolutionized the way goods and people moved across the world, drastically reshaping the global economy. Before the advent of steamships and the opening of the Suez Canal, maritime travel was largely dominated by sailing ships, which relied on the wind to propel them across oceans. These ships were often at the mercy of weather conditions and faced long, unpredictable journeys, especially when navigating through difficult waters like those around the southern tip of Africa. The Suez Canal and steamship technology dramatically changed this dynamic, ushering in an era of faster, more reliable, and more efficient transportation.

The advent of steam-powered vessels in the early 19th century began to revolutionize global shipping. Unlike sailing ships, steamships were not dependent on the wind, giving them greater control over their speed and routes. Steamships could maintain consistent speeds even in unfavorable weather, making them much more reliable for long-distance travel. This new technology was a game changer, especially for trade between Europe and Asia, two regions separated by vast distances and treacherous waters. The opening of the Suez Canal in 1869 provided an even greater boost to the burgeoning steamship industry. By cutting a direct route between the Mediterranean Sea and the Red Sea, the canal offered a shortcut that greatly reduced the travel time for ships moving between Europe and Asia. The combination of steamships and the Suez Canal fundamentally altered the maritime landscape, making global trade more efficient and profitable.

Before the Suez Canal, ships traveling between Europe and Asia had to navigate around the Cape of Good Hope at the southern tip of

Africa. This journey was long, dangerous, and expensive. It often took months to complete, depending on the winds and weather conditions, and it was common for ships to encounter rough seas or even be lost to storms. For centuries, this was the only viable sea route between Europe and Asia, but the age of steamships and the construction of the Suez Canal changed everything. With steamships, ships could travel much faster and with greater predictability, while the canal provided a direct route that cut out the need to sail around Africa altogether. The result was a dramatic reduction in travel times—steamships using the Suez Canal could now make the journey between Europe and Asia in a fraction of the time it once took sailing ships. This efficiency opened up new possibilities for trade, as merchants and companies could transport goods faster and more frequently than ever before.

The economic impact of these changes was profound. Steamships traveling through the Suez Canal allowed for the rapid movement of goods between Europe and Asia, making trade more lucrative for both regions. Goods such as spices, tea, textiles, and manufactured products could now be transported in bulk with far greater speed and reliability. The canal became a vital artery for global commerce, and steamships were the vessels that made it all possible. European powers, particularly Britain, quickly recognized the value of the Suez Canal for maintaining their colonial empires. Britain's vast holdings in India, for example, depended heavily on the canal for trade and communication. Steamships made regular trips through the canal, carrying goods, mail, and passengers between Europe and its colonial territories in Asia. The faster travel times meant that Britain could maintain closer control over its colonies and respond more quickly to events unfolding in its empire. The canal and steamships thus played a key role in sustaining European imperialism in the 19th and early 20th centuries.

The rise of steamship technology and the opening of the Suez Canal also had significant political implications. Control over the canal became a strategic priority for European powers, particularly Britain and France, who both had interests in maintaining their dominance in global trade and colonial expansion. The canal was initially built and operated by the French Suez Canal Company, but Britain quickly moved to secure its influence over the waterway. In 1875, Britain purchased a controlling interest in the Suez Canal Company from the financially struggling Egyptian government. This move gave Britain significant control over the canal and ensured that it would remain open to British steamships, which were vital for maintaining trade routes to India and other colonies. The canal became a critical lifeline for Britain's empire, and its importance only grew as steamships continued to dominate global shipping.

One of the major advantages of steamships during the age of the Suez Canal was their ability to carry larger loads of cargo compared to sailing ships. Steamships were not limited by the size of their sails or the need for favorable wind conditions, which allowed them to be constructed larger and more powerful. This capacity to carry more goods at once meant that merchants and shipping companies could move greater quantities of products between Europe and Asia, further fueling global trade. The Suez Canal, with its strategic location, allowed these large steamships to move efficiently between markets, reducing costs and maximizing profits. Shipping companies, in turn, invested heavily in steamship fleets to take full advantage of the canal, as the demand for faster and more frequent trade routes grew.

The relationship between the Suez Canal and the age of steamships was also a mutually beneficial one. While steamships gained an immense advantage from using the canal, the canal itself benefited from the growing popularity of steam-powered vessels. The steady flow of steamships through the canal generated substantial revenue for the Suez Canal Company, as each ship was required to pay tolls for passage. As steamships became the dominant form of maritime transport, the canal saw a dramatic increase in traffic, making it one of the busiest and most profitable waterways in the world. The income generated from steamships allowed the canal to expand and modernize over time, ensuring that it could accommodate the increasing number and size of ships passing through.

In addition to its economic and political significance, the Suez Canal and steamship era had profound social and cultural implications. The faster travel times afforded by steamships allowed for greater mobility of people between Europe and Asia. The canal became a major thoroughfare for passengers, not just goods, with steamships regularly carrying travelers, migrants, and military personnel between the continents. Wealthy Europeans could now embark on grand tours of Asia, exploring the cultures of India, China, and Japan, while colonial administrators and military officers could quickly travel to their posts in far-flung territories. Steamships also facilitated the migration of workers, particularly from Asia to other parts of the British Empire. Indian and Chinese laborers, for example, were transported in large numbers to British colonies in Africa, the Caribbean, and Southeast Asia, where they played a crucial role in the development of plantations, railroads, and other colonial infrastructure.

The age of steamships, combined with the Suez Canal, also had significant environmental consequences. Steamships were powered by coal, which required massive amounts of fuel to propel them across oceans. The demand for coal grew exponentially as steamships became the dominant form of maritime transport, leading to increased mining and extraction of coal resources around the world. The Suez Canal itself became a focal point for refueling steamships, as ships traveling through the canal needed to stop and replenish their coal supplies. This created a thriving coal industry in regions near the canal, particularly in Egypt, where ports such as Port Said and Suez became major centers for refueling steamships. However, the reliance on coal also had negative environmental effects, as coal-powered steamships emitted large amounts of pollution into the atmosphere and contributed to the degradation of air and water quality in port cities.

As the 19th century progressed, steamships continued to evolve, becoming larger, faster, and more efficient. Advances in shipbuilding technology, such as the development of iron and steel hulls, allowed for the construction of even more powerful steamships capable of carrying massive cargoes. These larger vessels could easily navigate the Suez Canal, making it even more important for global trade. The canal itself underwent several expansions and improvements to accommodate the growing size of steamships. Dredging operations were carried out to deepen and widen the canal, ensuring that it could handle the increasing volume of traffic. By the early 20th century, the Suez Canal was one of the busiest waterways in the world, with thousands of steamships passing through each year.

The connection between the Suez Canal and steamships continued into the 20th century, but new challenges began to emerge. The rise of oil-powered ships, which were more efficient and cleaner than coal-powered steamships, gradually displaced traditional steamships. These new ships still benefited from the Suez Canal, as it remained a critical link in global trade, but the age of coal-powered steamships began to decline. Despite this shift in technology, the legacy of the Suez Canal and steamships remained strong. The canal had firmly established itself as one of the most important waterways in the world, and steamships had played a central role in its success. Together, they had transformed global trade, connecting Europe, Asia, and Africa in ways that had never been possible before.

Today, the Suez Canal continues to be a vital artery for global commerce, though the age of steamships has long since passed. Modern ships, powered by oil and other advanced technologies, now dominate the maritime industry, but they owe much of their success to the innovations of the steamship era. The Suez Canal, which has undergone several expansions and upgrades since its opening, remains a critical passage for ships traveling between Europe and Asia. The canal's ability to accommodate larger and more advanced vessels ensures its continued relevance in the global economy, just as it did during the age of steamships. In many ways, the Suez Canal and the age of steamships represent the birth of the modern global economy, an economy that is interconnected, interdependent, and driven by the movement of goods and people across vast distances.

The age of steamships and the Suez Canal is a testament to human ingenuity and the power of technological progress. Together, they reshaped the world, making it smaller, more accessible, and more connected than ever before. While steamships have been replaced by newer technologies, the impact they had on global trade, travel, and transportation will never be forgotten. The Suez Canal, born in the age of steam, continues to play a central role in global commerce, carrying forward the legacy of the steamships that first sailed through its waters.

Chapter 7: The Suez Canal Company Story

The story of the Suez Canal Company is one of ambition, international collaboration, political intrigue, and the far-reaching effects of a groundbreaking project that transformed global trade. Founded in the mid-19th century, the Suez Canal Company emerged as the driving force behind the construction and operation of the Suez Canal, one of the most important engineering feats in history. Its formation, growth, and eventual dissolution span over a century, during which it played a pivotal role in shaping world commerce and influencing geopolitical dynamics. The company not only oversaw the creation of the canal but also became a symbol of the competing interests between nations, businesses, and empires that sought to control the lifeblood of international trade.

The roots of the Suez Canal Company can be traced back to the dream of Ferdinand de Lesseps, a French diplomat with a vision of linking the Mediterranean Sea with the Red Sea to shorten the maritime route between Europe and Asia. After obtaining permission from the Egyptian government, de Lesseps sought to turn his vision into reality by establishing a company to finance and construct the canal. In 1858, the Compagnie Universelle du Canal Maritime de Suez (Universal Suez Ship Canal Company) was officially formed, with de Lesseps at its helm. The company was headquartered in Paris, and its primary purpose was to raise the necessary funds, plan the construction, and manage the operation of the canal once completed.

From its inception, the Suez Canal Company faced significant challenges. Financing a project of such magnitude was no easy task, and the company needed to attract investors from across Europe. Although de Lesseps was successful in securing initial investments from French and Egyptian sources, there was considerable skepticism, particularly from the British, who were wary of French control over such a strategically vital waterway. At the time, Britain was the world's leading maritime power, and the prospect of a French-dominated Suez Canal raised concerns about potential interference with British trade routes to India and other colonies in Asia.

Despite these geopolitical tensions, the Suez Canal Company pressed forward with its mission. The company employed a workforce that included tens of thousands of Egyptian laborers and European engineers, all working under harsh conditions to dig the canal through the desert. The construction process was grueling, with workers facing extreme heat, disease, and difficult terrain. The use of forced labor, especially in the early stages, drew criticism from humanitarian groups and governments alike, but the Suez Canal Company, determined to complete the project, continued its efforts. After ten years of arduous work, the Suez Canal was finally completed in 1869, and the first ships sailed through the newly constructed waterway.

The opening of the canal was a monumental achievement for the Suez Canal Company, marking the beginning of a new era in global trade. The company quickly established itself as a powerful force in international commerce, as the canal became a vital shortcut for ships traveling between Europe and Asia. The canal dramatically reduced travel time, cutting thousands of miles from the journey around the southern tip of Africa. As a result, the Suez Canal Company reaped significant financial rewards from the tolls it charged ships for passage. The company collected tolls based on the tonnage of ships passing through, generating substantial profits and quickly becoming one of the most profitable companies of the era.

The success of the Suez Canal Company, however, was accompanied by increasing political tensions. The canal's strategic importance made it a focal point for rivalries between European powers, particularly France and Britain. Although the canal was technically located in Egypt, the Suez Canal Company maintained control over its operations, and by extension, the flow of goods through one of the world's most critical waterways. Britain, which had initially been skeptical of the canal, soon realized its value for maintaining trade routes to India, its most prized colony. As a result, the British government sought to gain greater influence over the canal and the Suez Canal Company.

In 1875, the British government, under Prime Minister Benjamin Disraeli, made a bold move to secure control over the canal. The Egyptian government, which had been a major shareholder in the Suez Canal Company, was facing a severe financial crisis and needed to sell its shares in the company to raise funds. Disraeli saw this as an opportunity and quickly arranged for Britain to purchase Egypt's shares in the Suez Canal Company for £4 million. This purchase gave Britain a controlling interest in the company, and by extension, significant influence over the canal's operations. The acquisition of the shares was seen as a major diplomatic victory for Britain and solidified its role as the dominant power in the Suez region.

With Britain now controlling the majority of the company's shares, the Suez Canal became even more critical to the maintenance of the British Empire. The canal served as the key maritime link between Britain and its colonies in Asia, allowing for the rapid movement of troops, goods, and communication. For the next several decades, the Suez Canal Company continued to operate under the influence of both British and French interests, although Britain held the upper hand due to its majority ownership. The company's profits soared as more and more ships used the canal, and the Suez Canal became an indispensable part of the global trading system.

The story of the Suez Canal Company, however, took a dramatic turn in the mid-20th century, when the canal and its controlling company became the center of a major international crisis. In the years following World War II, Egypt, under the leadership of President Gamal Abdel Nasser, sought to assert greater control over the canal, which was still operated by the Suez Canal Company. Nasser, who was determined to modernize Egypt and reduce foreign influence, viewed the canal as a symbol of colonial exploitation. In 1956, Nasser made a bold decision to nationalize the Suez Canal, effectively taking control of the canal from the Suez Canal Company. This move triggered the Suez Crisis, as Britain, France, and Israel launched a military intervention to regain control of the canal and protect their interests.

The Suez Crisis marked a turning point in the history of the Suez Canal Company. Although the military intervention initially succeeded in capturing the canal, international pressure, particularly from the United States and the Soviet Union, forced the invading powers to withdraw. Egypt retained control of the canal, and the Suez Canal Company's operations came to an end. The company was formally dissolved in 1958, and its assets were transferred to the Egyptian government. The nationalization of the canal marked the end of an era, as the Suez Canal Company, which had once been one of the most powerful and profitable companies in the world, was no more.

The dissolution of the Suez Canal Company did not mark the end of the canal's importance, however. Under Egyptian control, the canal continued to serve as a vital waterway for international trade. The Egyptian government took on the responsibility of maintaining and modernizing the canal, ensuring that it could accommodate the growing size of ships and the increasing volume of global trade. The revenue generated from the canal became an important source of income for Egypt, and the canal remains one of the country's most valuable assets to this day.

Looking back, the story of the Suez Canal Company is a testament to the power of vision and the influence of commerce on international relations. What began as a daring project spearheaded by a French diplomat evolved into a critical asset for global trade and a symbol of geopolitical rivalry. The company's ability to finance and complete the construction of the Suez Canal in the face of significant challenges was a remarkable achievement, one that transformed global shipping and forever altered the course of world history. The company's legacy lives on in the form of the Suez Canal itself, a waterway that continues to play a central role in the movement of goods and people between continents.

The Suez Canal Company's story is also a reminder of the complex interplay between business and politics. The company, though a commercial enterprise, became deeply entangled in the strategic interests of nations, particularly Britain and France. Its operations were shaped not only by the demands of global trade but also by the shifting power dynamics of empires and the rise of nationalism in the 20th century. The nationalization of the canal by Egypt was a turning point, highlighting the growing desire of formerly colonized nations to reclaim control over their resources and infrastructure.

In conclusion, the Suez Canal Company's story is a multifaceted one, encompassing engineering triumphs, international finance, political intrigue, and the enduring importance of maritime trade. From its founding in 1858 to its dissolution a century later, the company played a pivotal role in shaping the world economy and influencing the course of history. Its legacy is inextricably linked to the Suez Canal itself, a waterway that remains one of the most important and heavily trafficked routes in the world today. While the Suez Canal Company may no longer exist, the canal's continued operation stands as a testament to the vision and determination of those who first conceived of linking the Mediterranean and Red Seas, and to the complex story of the company that made that vision a reality.

Chapter 8: Nationalization of the Canal

The nationalization of the Suez Canal in 1956 was one of the most significant political and economic events of the 20th century, dramatically reshaping global power dynamics and marking a defining moment in the post-colonial world. It was an event that not only altered the control of one of the world's most vital waterways but also highlighted the aspirations of emerging nations in asserting their sovereignty and challenging the influence of former colonial powers. The nationalization, initiated by Egypt's President Gamal Abdel Nasser, was not only a matter of national pride for Egypt but also set off a chain of international events that led to the Suez Crisis—a military and diplomatic showdown that reflected the complex geopolitical landscape of the Cold War era. The decision to nationalize the canal had far-reaching consequences, impacting global trade, international relations, and the very nature of post-colonial governance.

In order to fully understand the nationalization of the Suez Canal, it is crucial to appreciate the historical context in which it took place. For nearly a century prior, the Suez Canal had been controlled by the Suez Canal Company, a powerful corporation dominated by French and British interests. Though the canal itself ran through Egyptian territory, Egypt had very little control over its operations and saw only limited financial benefit from its use. The British, in particular, viewed the canal as a critical asset for maintaining their empire, especially in terms of securing vital trade routes to India and the rest of Asia. After Britain purchased a controlling stake in the Suez Canal Company in 1875, the canal essentially became a British-controlled waterway, despite nominal Egyptian sovereignty over the land it crossed.

For decades, Egypt's lack of control over the canal became a source of frustration and national humiliation. By the mid-20th century, Egypt was in the midst of a transformative period under the leadership of Gamal Abdel Nasser, a charismatic and ambitious figure who had risen to power following the 1952 Egyptian revolution that overthrew the monarchy. Nasser was a passionate advocate of Arab nationalism and anti-imperialism, and his vision for Egypt was one of independence from foreign domination, particularly from the lingering influence of Britain and France. He sought to modernize Egypt's economy, strengthen its military, and position it as a leader in the Arab world. Central to Nasser's vision was the idea that Egypt should fully control its own resources, including the Suez Canal.

The spark that led to the nationalization of the canal was the collapse of negotiations between Egypt and Western powers over the financing of the Aswan High Dam, a massive infrastructure project that Nasser viewed as essential for Egypt's economic development. The dam, intended to regulate the flow of the Nile River and provide Egypt with much-needed hydroelectric power, was originally supposed to be funded by loans from the United States and Britain. However, in July 1956, the United States and Britain withdrew their financial support for the project, largely due to Nasser's growing ties with the Soviet Union and his refusal to align Egypt with the Western bloc during the Cold War. This withdrawal of support was a major blow to Nasser, but it also provided him with an opportunity to take bold action.

On July 26, 1956, in a dramatic and defiant move, Nasser announced that Egypt was nationalizing the Suez Canal. He declared that the canal would be placed under Egyptian control and that the revenue generated from its tolls would be used to finance the construction of the Aswan High Dam. Nasser's speech, delivered in Alexandria to a massive and enthusiastic crowd, became a symbol of Egypt's determination to assert its sovereignty and break free from foreign influence. In the speech, Nasser invoked the memory of Ferdinand de Lesseps, the Frenchman who had overseen the construction of the canal, using Lesseps' name as a secret codeword to initiate the nationalization. As Nasser spoke, Egyptian troops and workers swiftly moved to take control of the canal and the offices of the Suez Canal Company.

The nationalization of the canal was met with widespread jubilation in Egypt and across the Arab world. For many Egyptians, the canal had long been a symbol of foreign exploitation, and Nasser's bold action was seen as a triumph of national sovereignty. It also resonated with other nations that had experienced colonial rule, as it demonstrated that a post-colonial nation could successfully reclaim control over its own assets. Nasser became a hero in the eyes of many, not just in Egypt but across the Arab world and in other developing nations.

However, the nationalization of the canal also set off a firestorm of international controversy. Britain and France, both of which had significant economic and strategic interests in the canal, were outraged by Nasser's actions. The canal was a critical artery for global trade, particularly for the transportation of oil from the Middle East to Europe, and its sudden nationalization by Egypt was seen as a direct threat to Western economic interests. The British government, led by Prime Minister Anthony Eden, viewed Nasser's actions as an unacceptable challenge to British authority and prestige. France, which had its own colonial interests in North Africa and was dealing with a rebellion in Algeria, also saw Nasser's move as a dangerous precedent for anti-colonial movements. Both Britain and France feared that allowing Nasser to retain control of the canal would embolden other nationalist movements and weaken their influence in the Middle East and beyond.

In response, Britain and France sought to regain control of the canal through diplomatic and, eventually, military means. Behind the scenes, they began planning a coordinated military intervention, and they soon found an ally in Israel, which was eager to strike at Egypt due to its ongoing conflicts with Nasser's regime. The result was the infamous Suez Crisis, also known as the Suez War. In late October

1956, Israeli forces invaded the Sinai Peninsula, advancing toward the canal. Shortly thereafter, Britain and France issued an ultimatum to both Egypt and Israel, demanding that they cease hostilities and withdraw from the canal zone. When Nasser refused, British and French forces launched a military invasion, bombing Egyptian positions and landing troops near the canal.

The military intervention, however, did not go as planned. While British and French forces initially achieved some military success, the international response to their actions was overwhelmingly negative. Both the United States and the Soviet Union condemned the invasion, albeit for different reasons. U.S. President Dwight D. Eisenhower, concerned about the potential for a wider conflict and the impact on American influence in the Middle East, pressured Britain and France to halt their military operations. Eisenhower was also deeply concerned about the damage the invasion could do to Western relations with newly independent nations in the developing world. The Soviet Union, meanwhile, saw the crisis as an opportunity to increase its influence in the Middle East and offered its support to Nasser.

Faced with mounting international pressure and condemnation, Britain, France, and Israel were forced to withdraw their forces from Egypt. The United Nations intervened to broker a ceasefire, and a U.N. peacekeeping force was deployed to the region to supervise the withdrawal and ensure the reopening of the canal, which had been temporarily closed due to the conflict. Nasser emerged from the crisis as a victorious figure, having successfully stood up to two of the world's most powerful colonial powers. The canal remained under Egyptian control, and Nasser's reputation as a champion of Arab nationalism and anti-imperialism was solidified.

The nationalization of the Suez Canal and the subsequent Suez Crisis marked a turning point in global politics. For Egypt, it was a moment of immense national pride, symbolizing the country's newfound independence and control over its own destiny. For Britain and France, the crisis was a humiliating blow, signaling the end of their imperial dominance in the region and marking the beginning of their decline as global powers. The Suez Crisis also demonstrated the changing dynamics of the Cold War, as the United States and the Soviet Union both sought to expand their influence in the Middle East.

In the years following the nationalization, Egypt continued to operate the Suez Canal, which became a major source of revenue for the country. The canal's importance to global trade only increased in the decades that followed, particularly with the growing demand for oil. While Nasser's dream of fully financing the Aswan High Dam with canal revenues was not entirely realized, the canal nonetheless played a critical role in Egypt's economy and its relations with the wider world.

The nationalization of the Suez Canal remains a defining moment in modern history, not only for Egypt but for the entire post-colonial world. It was an event that challenged the established order of imperial control and demonstrated the power of nationalism in reshaping global politics. Nasser's bold move to take control of the canal sent a powerful message to other nations that had experienced colonial rule: that they, too, could reclaim control over their own resources and chart their own course in the international arena. The Suez Canal, once a symbol of foreign domination, became a symbol of Egyptian sovereignty and independence, and its nationalization continues to be remembered as a key moment in the global struggle for self-determination.

Chapter 9: The Suez Crisis of 1956

The Suez Crisis of 1956, also known as the Second Arab-Israeli War or the Tripartite Aggression, was one of the most dramatic geopolitical events of the 20th century, reshaping the post-World War II global order and marking a significant turning point in the history of imperialism and nationalism. The crisis, centered on the Suez Canal—a vital waterway linking the Mediterranean Sea to the Red Sea—had wide-ranging consequences for the Middle East, Europe, the United States, and the Soviet Union. It not only exposed the declining influence of European colonial powers but also underscored the growing strategic importance of the Middle East during the Cold War. The Suez Crisis was a convergence of conflicting interests among multiple players, including Egypt, Britain, France, Israel, the United States, and the Soviet Union, and its ramifications were felt across the world.

The roots of the Suez Crisis can be traced to a variety of factors, the most prominent being Egyptian President Gamal Abdel Nasser's decision to nationalize the Suez Canal on July 26, 1956. The canal, which had been built under the supervision of French diplomat Ferdinand de Lesseps in the 19th century, was one of the most strategically and economically important waterways in the world. For decades, the canal had been controlled by the Suez Canal Company, a multinational corporation dominated by British and French interests, even though it ran through Egyptian territory. The canal was crucial to global trade, particularly for the transportation of oil from the Middle East to Europe. At the time of the crisis, two-thirds of Europe's oil supply passed through the Suez Canal, making it a lifeline for Western economies.

Nasser's nationalization of the canal was a bold and provocative move, but it was also driven by broader geopolitical dynamics. Since coming to power in 1952 after a military coup that ousted Egypt's monarchy, Nasser had emerged as a leading figure in the Arab world and a vocal advocate of Arab nationalism. He sought to rid Egypt of foreign influence, particularly that of the British, who still maintained a military presence in the Suez Canal Zone even after granting Egypt nominal independence. Nasser's ultimate goal was to modernize Egypt and assert its sovereignty on the world stage, and he saw the canal as both a symbol of foreign domination and a vital asset that could be used to finance Egypt's development.

At the heart of Nasser's development plans was the construction of the Aswan High Dam, a massive hydroelectric project intended to provide Egypt with much-needed electricity and regulate the flow of the Nile River. Nasser initially sought financial assistance from the United States and Britain to fund the project, but the negotiations ultimately broke down. The withdrawal of Western support for the dam was partly due to Nasser's growing ties with the Soviet Union, as Egypt sought to maintain a neutral stance in the Cold War. In response to the loss of Western funding, Nasser made the dramatic decision to nationalize the Suez Canal, declaring that the revenue from canal tolls would be used to finance the dam. The nationalization was a deeply symbolic act of defiance against colonial powers, and it resonated across the Arab world as a victory for anti-imperialism.

Nasser's nationalization of the canal was met with outrage in Britain and France, both of which had significant economic and strategic interests in the waterway. For Britain, the canal was the key to maintaining its dwindling empire, particularly its trade routes to India and other parts of Asia. British Prime Minister Anthony Eden viewed Nasser as a dangerous figure who was undermining British influence in the region, and he compared Nasser to European dictators like Mussolini and Hitler. For France, Nasser's actions were seen as a direct threat to its colonial holdings, particularly in Algeria, where a brutal war of independence was underway. The French government feared that Nasser's pan-Arab nationalist ideology would inspire anti-colonial movements across North Africa and beyond. As a result, both Britain and France began to seek ways to reverse Nasser's nationalization of the canal and restore their control over the waterway.

At the same time, Israel had its own reasons for viewing Nasser as a threat. Since its founding in 1948, Israel had been locked in a bitter and violent conflict with its Arab neighbors, including Egypt. Nasser's vocal opposition to Israel and his support for Palestinian resistance movements had further strained relations between the two nations. In the years leading up to the Suez Crisis, cross-border skirmishes between Israeli and Egyptian forces had become increasingly frequent, and Nasser had imposed a blockade on Israeli shipping through the Straits of Tiran, cutting off Israel's access to the Red Sea. Israel saw Nasser's growing influence and military buildup as an existential threat, and the nationalization of the canal only heightened these concerns.

In response to Nasser's nationalization, Britain, France, and Israel secretly devised a military plan to take back control of the canal and weaken Nasser's regime. Known as the Sevres Protocol, the plan called for Israel to launch a military invasion of the Sinai Peninsula, advancing toward the Suez Canal. Britain and France would then issue an ultimatum, calling for a ceasefire and demanding that both Egypt and Israel withdraw from the canal zone. When Nasser inevitably refused, British and French forces would intervene, ostensibly as peacekeepers, to take control of the canal and topple Nasser. The plan was kept secret from the United States, which was not consulted and did not support military intervention.

On October 29, 1956, the first phase of the plan was put into action when Israeli forces invaded the Sinai Peninsula. In a swift and well-coordinated military operation, Israeli troops advanced toward the Suez Canal, capturing key Egyptian positions along the way. Two days later, on October 31, Britain and France issued their ultimatum, demanding a halt to the fighting and threatening to intervene if Egypt did not comply. As expected, Nasser rejected the ultimatum, and

British and French forces began their military intervention. On November 5, British and French paratroopers landed near the canal, and naval forces bombarded Egyptian positions in an attempt to secure the waterway.

However, the military intervention did not go as smoothly as Britain and France had hoped. While their forces were able to achieve some tactical success on the ground, the invasion provoked a massive international outcry. The United States, under President Dwight D. Eisenhower, was furious at being kept in the dark about the plan and strongly opposed the use of force. Eisenhower's administration feared that the invasion would destabilize the Middle East, alienate Arab nations, and potentially drive them into the arms of the Soviet Union. At the height of the Cold War, the U.S. was keen to avoid any escalation of tensions in the region that might lead to a broader conflict.

The Soviet Union, for its part, condemned the invasion in the strongest terms and threatened to intervene on behalf of Egypt. Soviet Premier Nikita Khrushchev issued a series of ominous warnings, including a threat to launch missile strikes against Britain and France if they did not cease their military operations. The Soviet Union also took the issue to the United Nations, calling for an immediate halt to the hostilities and the withdrawal of British, French, and Israeli forces from Egypt.

Faced with mounting pressure from both the United States and the Soviet Union, Britain and France found themselves increasingly isolated on the world stage. Eisenhower, determined to end the crisis, took the unprecedented step of using American economic leverage to force Britain and France to back down. The U.S. threatened to impose financial sanctions on Britain, which was already struggling with economic difficulties in the aftermath of World War II. Faced with the prospect of a financial crisis and diplomatic isolation, Eden reluctantly agreed to a ceasefire, and British and French forces began to withdraw from Egypt.

The Suez Crisis officially ended on November 7, 1956, when a ceasefire was declared and hostilities came to a halt. In the aftermath of the crisis, a United Nations peacekeeping force was deployed to the region to supervise the withdrawal of foreign troops and ensure the reopening of the canal, which had been temporarily closed due to the conflict. Nasser, who had emerged as the hero of the crisis, retained control of the canal, and Egypt's sovereignty over the waterway was affirmed. The canal was reopened to shipping in early 1957, and Nasser's status as a champion of Arab nationalism and anti-imperialism was cemented.

The Suez Crisis had far-reaching consequences for the global balance of power. For Britain and France, the crisis marked the beginning of the end of their roles as dominant colonial powers. The humiliating failure of their military intervention exposed the limits of their influence and signaled a shift in the global order, as the United States and the Soviet Union emerged as the two dominant superpowers in the post-World War II era. In Britain, the crisis led to the resignation of Prime Minister Anthony Eden, who was widely criticized for his handling of the situation. France, meanwhile, continued to grapple with its colonial wars in Algeria and Indochina, but the Suez Crisis underscored the diminishing ability of European powers to maintain their empires in the face of nationalist movements.

For Egypt and the broader Arab world, the Suez Crisis was a defining moment of triumph. Nasser's successful resistance against the combined forces of Britain, France, and Israel was seen as a victory for Arab nationalism and a rejection of Western imperialism. Nasser became a symbol of Arab unity and anti-colonialism, and his influence in the region grew significantly in the years that followed. The crisis also had a profound impact on the wider Middle East, contributing to the rise of Arab nationalism and the increasing importance of oil as a geopolitical weapon in the decades to come.

On the global stage, the Suez Crisis demonstrated the changing dynamics of the Cold War. It showed that the United States, despite being allied with Britain and France in NATO, was willing to oppose its European allies in order to maintain stability in the Middle East and prevent Soviet expansion. The crisis also highlighted the effectiveness of the United Nations as a forum for resolving international disputes, as the organization played a key role in brokering the ceasefire and overseeing the withdrawal of foreign forces.

In conclusion, the Suez Crisis of 1956 was a watershed moment in 20th-century history, marking the decline of European colonialism, the rise of Arab nationalism, and the growing importance of the Middle East in global geopolitics. It exposed the fragility of imperial powers, reshaped the postwar world order, and set the stage for future conflicts and power struggles in the region. The crisis also underscored the strategic importance of the Suez Canal, which remains one of the most vital waterways in the world to this day.

Chapter 10: The Canal in Wartime

Throughout its history, the Suez Canal has been a crucial strategic asset, not just as a commercial waterway linking Europe and Asia but also as a key military chokepoint. Its unique position, connecting the Mediterranean Sea to the Red Sea, has meant that the canal has played a pivotal role during times of war. Wars of empire, world wars, and regional conflicts have all impacted the canal in various ways, with powers fighting over its control or using it for military operations. Whether as an objective for conquest, a battleground, or a tool for cutting off supply lines, the Suez Canal's significance in wartime has shaped not only the history of Egypt but also the broader geopolitical landscape of the Middle East and beyond.

The Suez Canal's military importance was evident even during its early years, but it became especially clear in the late 19th century, soon after its opening in 1869. European imperial powers, particularly Britain, understood the canal's vital role in maintaining their global influence and colonial empires. For the British, the Suez Canal was the linchpin of their route to India, the crown jewel of their empire. As such, control of the canal became a critical aspect of British military and diplomatic strategy. Even though the canal was technically neutral under international agreements, its geographic location meant that whoever controlled Egypt could effectively control access to the waterway. This reality would shape the canal's wartime role for many decades.

During World War I, the Suez Canal quickly became a focal point of military activity. The canal's importance to the British Empire was undeniable, as it provided the quickest route to its colonies and resources in Asia and Africa. The Ottoman Empire, which had joined the Central Powers, sought to disrupt the British war effort by targeting the canal. In 1915, Ottoman forces launched a direct assault on the Suez Canal, hoping to cut off British supply lines and weaken their position in the region. The attack, known as the First Suez Offensive, was a significant military engagement. However, British forces, aided by Indian colonial troops, successfully repelled the Ottomans. The defense of the canal was crucial, as it allowed the British to maintain their dominance in the Middle East and safeguard their access to vital resources. The canal also became an essential supply route for the movement of troops, weapons, and supplies between Europe and the colonies.

World War I demonstrated the canal's vulnerability in times of war, and it prompted the British to further entrench their control over Egypt. Despite Egypt's formal status as part of the Ottoman Empire, Britain had effectively made it a protectorate in 1882, and after the war, it strengthened its military presence in the canal zone. British forces stationed in Egypt played a crucial role in guarding the canal against potential threats, not only from regional powers but also from rival European nations. The Suez Canal, as both a strategic asset and a symbol of British imperial power, continued to be heavily militarized throughout the interwar period.

The canal's strategic importance reached new heights during World War II. By this time, control of the Suez Canal was not just a matter of imperial prestige—it was a matter of life and death for the Allied war effort. The British Empire was under siege on multiple fronts, and the canal was a critical lifeline for moving troops, supplies, and oil between Europe, the Middle East, and the Far East. During the war, the canal became a target of repeated attacks by the Axis powers, particularly Nazi Germany and its ally, Italy. German Field Marshal Erwin Rommel, commanding the Afrika Korps, made a determined push to capture Egypt and seize control of the canal in 1942. The ensuing battles in North Africa, particularly the Battle of El Alamein, were among the most pivotal of the war. Had Rommel's forces succeeded in taking the canal, the consequences for the Allies would have been disastrous. The loss of the canal would have severely hampered the Allied ability to project power in the Middle East and Asia, cutting off vital supply routes and allowing Axis forces to dominate the region.

However, British and Allied forces, under the command of General Bernard Montgomery, were able to defeat Rommel in the decisive Second Battle of El Alamein. This victory not only secured the Suez Canal but also marked a turning point in the North African campaign, eventually leading to the withdrawal of Axis forces from the region. The defense of the canal during World War II solidified its status as a critical asset in the global balance of power. It also demonstrated that the canal, though not directly a battlefield, was always a key military target due to its impact on global logistics and supply chains. The experience of World War II further entrenched the British military presence in Egypt, as the canal remained vital to Britain's post-war strategic interests.

The post-war period, however, would soon see the canal embroiled in a different kind of conflict—one rooted in the rising tide of Arab nationalism and decolonization. As Britain and France sought to maintain their influence in the Middle East, local leaders like Egypt's President Gamal Abdel Nasser sought to assert control over their own countries and resources, including the Suez Canal. Nasser's nationalization of the canal in 1956, and the subsequent Suez Crisis, marked one of the most significant wartime events in the canal's history. While the 1956 conflict was not a world war, it was a critical flashpoint in the Cold War and signaled the decline of European colonial powers in the region.

During the Suez Crisis, Israel, Britain, and France launched a military invasion of Egypt in response to Nasser's nationalization of the canal. Their goal was to regain control of the canal and remove Nasser from power. However, the intervention sparked widespread international condemnation, particularly from the United States and the Soviet Union, both of which were keen to prevent the conflict from escalating. While the military invasion initially went well for the tripartite alliance, they faced increasing political pressure to withdraw, and ultimately, the United Nations intervened to broker a ceasefire. The Suez Crisis exposed the canal's ongoing importance as a military asset and a geopolitical prize, but it also marked the end of Britain and France's ability to use military force to secure their interests in the region.

In the decades following the Suez Crisis, the canal continued to play a central role in regional conflicts, particularly during the Arab-Israeli wars. In the Six-Day War of 1967, Israel captured the Sinai Peninsula, bringing its forces to the eastern bank of the canal. As a result, the canal was effectively closed to international shipping for eight years, from 1967 to 1975, as the waterway became a de facto front line between Egyptian and Israeli forces. The War of Attrition, which took place from 1967 to 1970, saw repeated clashes between the two sides along the canal, with both Egyptian and Israeli artillery and air strikes targeting each other's positions. The canal, once a bustling artery of global trade, was transformed into a heavily militarized zone, with much of the surrounding area littered with mines and unexploded ordnance.

The most dramatic military engagement involving the canal occurred during the Yom Kippur War of 1973. In a surprise attack on October 6, 1973, Egyptian forces, under the command of President Anwar Sadat, launched a coordinated assault on Israeli positions along the canal. Crossing the waterway in the early hours of the morning, Egyptian soldiers successfully breached Israel's defenses, catching the Israeli military off guard. The initial Egyptian gains were a significant morale boost for the Arab world, as they temporarily reversed the humiliating losses of the 1967 war. However, the Israeli military quickly regrouped and counterattacked, eventually crossing the canal themselves and encircling the Egyptian Third Army. The war ended in a stalemate, but the canal once again proved to be a critical battleground in the broader Arab-Israeli conflict.

Following the 1973 war, the Suez Canal was reopened in 1975 after extensive negotiations and the signing of peace agreements between Egypt and Israel. The canal, which had been closed for nearly a decade, was dredged and cleared of mines, allowing for the resumption of international shipping. The reopening of the canal marked a new chapter in its history, as Egypt sought to restore the waterway's role as a vital artery of global trade. However, the wars of the 20th century had left a lasting legacy on the canal, with both the physical infrastructure and the surrounding region bearing the scars of decades of conflict.

In the years since, the canal has remained an important military asset, even as it has primarily functioned as a commercial waterway. Egypt, under successive governments, has maintained a strong military presence along the canal, recognizing its strategic importance. The canal has also continued to be a key factor in regional security calculations, particularly in the context of broader Middle East conflicts. As the world's dependence on Middle Eastern oil has grown, the canal's role as a chokepoint in global energy supplies has made it a potential flashpoint for future conflicts.

In conclusion, the Suez Canal's role in wartime has been one of constant strategic importance. From the Ottoman Empire's failed attempt to capture it in World War I to the critical battles of World War II, and the intense Arab-Israeli conflicts of the 20th century, the canal has been at the center of military and geopolitical struggles. Its significance goes far beyond being just a waterway for commerce—it is a symbol of power, control, and influence, shaping the course of world history through war and peace. Even today, the canal's military relevance endures, as its control remains essential for any nation seeking to exert dominance in the region.

Chapter 11: Expanding the Suez Canal

The expansion of the Suez Canal is one of the most significant engineering projects in modern history, aimed at bolstering the canal's capacity to handle an increasing volume of global maritime trade and to enhance its strategic importance. Throughout its existence, the Suez Canal has been a key artery for international commerce, enabling ships to bypass the long and dangerous journey around the southern tip of Africa, dramatically shortening the distance between Europe and Asia. However, as global trade has surged, especially with the rise of container shipping and larger vessels, the canal faced the challenge of becoming insufficient for modern needs. This led to several ambitious projects to expand and modernize the canal, culminating in the most dramatic transformation in the 21st century.

The Suez Canal, when it first opened in 1869, was already a marvel of engineering, but it was designed to accommodate the ships of that era, which were much smaller and fewer in number compared to today's global fleet. Over time, with the rapid industrialization of the world and the expansion of international trade, the canal became a vital thoroughfare for goods, raw materials, and energy supplies, particularly oil. As early as the late 19th and early 20th centuries, it became clear that the canal needed upgrades to keep pace with technological advances in shipping. The first expansions took place incrementally, such as widening and deepening the canal to allow for larger vessels and two-way traffic in certain sections. However, these improvements were modest compared to the later, more transformative projects.

By the mid-20th century, the canal was being used by increasingly larger ships, many of them carrying oil from the Middle East to Europe and beyond. The canal's narrow width and relatively shallow depth began to pose significant challenges for modern shipping, particularly as oil tankers grew in size. Following the nationalization of the canal in 1956 and the Suez Crisis, Egypt took over full control of the waterway, and with it, the responsibility for its maintenance and modernization. The canal was partially modernized during the 1960s and 1970s, especially after it was reopened in 1975 following its closure during the Arab-Israeli conflicts. These improvements allowed for a greater number of ships to pass through, but by the late 20th century, new pressures were mounting.

The growth of container shipping in the 1970s and 1980s, along with the increasing size of ships, created a need for more comprehensive expansion efforts. Ships were getting bigger, and their drafts (the depth of the water needed for a ship to float) were increasing, meaning that the canal's existing dimensions were becoming a constraint on the world's busiest trade routes. Larger vessels, such as supertankers and ultra-large container ships, could not pass through the canal fully loaded, and many had to offload cargo to smaller vessels to transit, reducing efficiency and increasing costs. This situation, combined with increasing global trade, pushed Egypt to consider a more substantial expansion.

By the early 21st century, it was clear that an even more dramatic overhaul of the canal was necessary to meet the demands of global trade. In 2014, Egypt's then-President Abdel Fattah el-Sisi announced an ambitious project to expand the Suez Canal. This expansion was part of a broader vision to boost Egypt's economy, create jobs, and reinforce the country's strategic importance on the world stage. The project, named the New Suez Canal, involved not only widening and deepening parts of the existing canal but also constructing a parallel waterway that would allow for two-way traffic along much of the canal's length. This new canal would significantly increase the capacity and speed of the waterway, allowing more ships to transit simultaneously and reducing waiting times.

The New Suez Canal project, completed in just one year, was an impressive feat of modern engineering. It involved the excavation of 35 kilometers of new waterway parallel to the existing canal and the widening and deepening of a further 37 kilometers of the original canal. The total length of the expanded canal was about 72 kilometers, and the project required the removal of over 250 million cubic meters of earth. The expansion allowed for the transit of larger ships, including those with a draft of up to 66 feet, and increased the canal's capacity to handle the world's largest vessels. The project also reduced transit times significantly, cutting the average passage time from 18 hours to 11 hours and increasing the number of ships that could pass through the canal daily from 49 to 97. This improvement not only made the canal more efficient but also more attractive to shipping companies, which now faced fewer delays and lower costs.

The Suez Canal expansion was a significant investment for Egypt, with the total cost of the project estimated at around $8.5 billion. The project was financed through the sale of investment certificates to Egyptian citizens, raising billions of dollars within a few days, reflecting the national importance of the canal. For Egypt, the expansion was not just about boosting global trade; it was also about cementing its role as a global hub for shipping and logistics. The canal is a major source of revenue for the Egyptian government, generating billions of dollars annually from tolls paid by ships passing through. The expanded canal was expected to double these revenues in the coming years, providing a much-needed boost to the Egyptian economy.

However, the expansion of the Suez Canal was not without its challenges. Critics argued that the project was rushed and that the expected economic benefits were overly optimistic. While the canal's expansion undoubtedly improved its capacity and efficiency, global shipping trends and economic conditions, such as fluctuations in oil prices and changes in trade routes, also play a significant role in determining the canal's long-term profitability. Additionally, the rise of alternative trade routes, such as the Northern Sea Route through the Arctic, which is becoming more accessible due to climate change, presents a potential challenge to the Suez Canal's dominance in global shipping.

Despite these challenges, the expanded Suez Canal has had a profound impact on global trade. It has allowed for the passage of some of the world's largest ships, including the massive container vessels that now dominate international commerce. The canal's increased capacity has also made it a critical component of the global supply chain, ensuring the smooth and timely movement of goods between Europe, Asia, and beyond. The expansion has also positioned Egypt as a key player in the global economy, with the canal serving as a gateway for international trade and a source of national pride.

In addition to the economic and strategic benefits, the Suez Canal expansion has had broader implications for global shipping. The ability to accommodate larger vessels has made the canal more attractive to shipping companies, which increasingly favor the economies of scale offered by ultra-large container ships. These massive vessels can carry thousands of containers, reducing the cost per unit of goods transported and making global trade more efficient. The expanded canal has thus become a vital link in the global logistics network, facilitating the movement of goods on an unprecedented scale.

The Suez Canal's expansion also reflects broader trends in the shipping industry, which has seen a continuous increase in the size of vessels over the past few decades. As global trade volumes have risen, particularly with the growth of China and other emerging economies, shipping companies have invested in ever-larger vessels to meet demand. The Suez Canal's expansion was a necessary response to these changes, ensuring that it could continue to accommodate the largest ships and maintain its position as one of the world's most important waterways.

Looking to the future, the Suez Canal is likely to remain a critical part of the global trading system. However, its long-term success will depend on a range of factors, including global economic conditions, shipping trends, and geopolitical developments. Egypt has already taken steps to ensure that the canal remains competitive, including ongoing maintenance and dredging to keep it navigable for the largest ships. There are also plans to develop the surrounding area into a major industrial and logistics hub, which could further enhance the canal's importance as a center of global trade.

In conclusion, the expansion of the Suez Canal represents a remarkable achievement in modern engineering and a crucial investment in the future of global commerce. The canal's ability to accommodate the world's largest ships has reinforced its status as a vital artery of international trade, while also boosting Egypt's economy and strategic importance. However, the canal's success will continue to depend on its ability to adapt to changing global conditions and to compete with alternative trade routes. As one of the world's most famous and strategically important waterways, the Suez Canal will likely remain a key player in global shipping for decades to come, its expanded capacity ensuring its continued relevance in an ever-evolving world.

Chapter 12: Life Along the Canal

Life along the Suez Canal has been shaped by its historical, economic, and geographical importance, creating a unique and ever-evolving environment for the people who live near this great waterway. For more than 150 years, the canal has been a vital artery for global trade, connecting the Mediterranean Sea with the Red Sea, but it is also much more than just a transportation route. The communities, industries, and ecosystems that thrive along the canal have been deeply influenced by its presence, creating a distinct way of life that reflects the intertwined nature of commerce, culture, and the natural world.

When the Suez Canal was completed in 1869, it dramatically changed the fortunes of the region. Before the canal, the Isthmus of Suez was largely a barren desert, sparsely populated and with limited economic activity. However, the opening of the canal transformed the area into a bustling hub of commerce, attracting workers, traders, and travelers from all over the world. Cities like Port Said, Ismailia, and Suez, which sit at key points along the canal, grew rapidly as they became important ports and centers of trade. This development spurred economic growth, creating jobs in shipping, logistics, and related industries, as well as in the construction and maintenance of the canal itself.

For the people living along the canal, daily life became closely tied to the rhythms of global commerce. The arrival and departure of ships, the movement of goods, and the presence of international visitors brought a sense of constant activity and connection to the wider world. In cities like Port Said, the canal's northern entrance, the population grew as immigrants from different parts of Egypt and the Mediterranean region arrived to seek opportunities in the new economy. Port Said became a cosmopolitan city, known for its cultural diversity and its role as a gateway between Europe, Africa, and Asia. The canal's proximity also brought foreign influence, as many of the engineers, technicians, and merchants who worked on or near the canal came from Europe, particularly France and Britain, during the early years of the canal's operation.

Ismailia, located about halfway along the canal, became another focal point of life along the waterway. Originally established as the headquarters for the construction of the canal, the city grew into a center of administration and culture. Its tree-lined streets, parks, and colonial-era architecture reflected the influence of the European engineers and administrators who lived there during the canal's early years. Ismailia's strategic location meant that it became a key hub for managing canal traffic and ensuring the smooth operation of the waterway. Over time, the city's population expanded, and it developed a unique identity as a blend of Egyptian and European influences, with its economy largely tied to the canal.

Suez, at the southern end of the canal, also developed into a significant port city. Suez had long been an important trade route for goods moving between the Red Sea and the Mediterranean, even before the canal was built. However, the completion of the canal transformed the city into a key point for international shipping, particularly for the transport of oil from the Middle East to Europe. The growth of the oil industry, in particular, had a major impact on life in Suez, as refineries and shipping companies established a presence in the area, providing employment and economic opportunities for the local population.

For the people living along the canal, the presence of this massive waterway has meant not only economic opportunities but also unique challenges. One of the most significant challenges has been the impact of political and military conflicts on the region. The Suez Canal has been at the center of numerous conflicts over the years, including the Suez Crisis of 1956, when Egypt nationalized the canal, and the Arab-Israeli wars, which led to the canal being closed from 1967 to 1975. During these periods, life along the canal was disrupted, with cities like Ismailia and Suez suffering from bombings, military occupation, and the displacement of residents. The closure of the canal during the Arab-Israeli conflicts had a profound effect on the local economy, as many businesses that relied on shipping and trade were forced to close or relocate.

Despite these challenges, the communities along the canal have demonstrated remarkable resilience. After the canal was reopened in 1975, the Egyptian government invested heavily in rebuilding and modernizing the cities and infrastructure along the waterway. The economy of the region gradually recovered, and the canal once again became a vital lifeline for international trade. Today, life along the canal is closely tied to its role as a global trade route, with many residents working in industries related to shipping, logistics, and oil production. The canal is also a major source of revenue for Egypt, generating billions of dollars annually in tolls from the ships that pass through, and much of this wealth flows into the local economy.

In addition to the economic aspects of life along the canal, the natural environment of the region has also been shaped by the presence of the waterway. Before the canal was built, the Isthmus of Suez was a desert region with little vegetation and few water sources. However, the creation of the canal brought a new source of water to the area, and with it, new opportunities for agriculture and settlement. Irrigation systems were developed to bring water from the canal to nearby farmland, allowing crops such as cotton, wheat, and fruits to be grown in areas that were previously too arid for cultivation. This development of agriculture along the canal provided food and livelihoods for the local population and helped to transform the region into a more habitable and productive area.

However, the canal's impact on the environment has not been entirely positive. The creation of the canal opened a new passageway between the Mediterranean Sea and the Red Sea, which had previously been separated by the land barrier of the isthmus. This connection allowed marine species from the Red Sea to enter the Mediterranean, a phenomenon known as "Lessepsian migration" after Ferdinand de Lesseps, the canal's chief engineer. Over time, species such as jellyfish, lionfish, and invasive seaweeds have spread into the Mediterranean, disrupting local ecosystems and causing challenges for fishermen and coastal communities. The introduction of these species has altered the marine biodiversity of the region, and efforts are ongoing to manage the environmental impact of the canal.

For the people who live near the Suez Canal, the waterway is also a source of fascination and pride. The sight of massive ships from around the world passing through the canal is a daily occurrence for many residents, and the canal has become a symbol of Egypt's strategic importance and engineering prowess. Tourists often visit cities like Ismailia and Port Said to see the canal up close, and local businesses cater to visitors who are drawn to the region's history and significance. In addition, the canal has played a role in shaping the cultural identity of the region. Festivals, celebrations, and local traditions often reflect the canal's importance, with many residents viewing it as a key part of their heritage.

The construction and expansion of the canal have also had a profound effect on the infrastructure of the region. Roads, bridges, and tunnels have been built to connect the cities and towns along the canal, making it easier for people and goods to move between the Mediterranean and the Red Sea coasts. The development of these transportation networks has facilitated trade and commerce not only within Egypt but also between Egypt and its neighbors. The canal has become a central artery for the movement of goods and people, linking Africa, Europe, and Asia in a way that has shaped the geography and economy of the region for generations.

Looking ahead, the future of life along the canal is likely to continue evolving as the global economy changes. The recent expansion of the canal, completed in 2015, has further increased its capacity to handle larger ships and more traffic, ensuring that it remains a critical part of the world's shipping network. As global trade continues to grow, the cities along the canal may see further development and investment, with new industries and technologies emerging to support the region's role as a hub of international commerce. At the same time, environmental and geopolitical challenges will continue to shape the region, as climate change, political instability, and shifts in global trade patterns impact the future of the canal and the communities that depend on it.

In conclusion, life along the Suez Canal is a complex and dynamic story of economic opportunity, cultural diversity, environmental change, and geopolitical significance. The canal has transformed the region from a sparsely populated desert into a thriving hub of global trade, bringing prosperity to its cities and shaping the lives of the people who live there. At the same time, the canal's impact on the environment and its role in global conflicts have created challenges that the region continues to navigate. For the people living along the canal, it is not just a waterway but a vital part of their identity, their economy, and their future.

Chapter 13: How the Canal Works Today

The Suez Canal, a vital artery of global trade, operates today as one of the most important and heavily trafficked waterways in the world. Its strategic importance is undeniable, as it serves as a direct route for ships traveling between Europe, Asia, and the Middle East, dramatically reducing the time and distance required for vessels to navigate these regions. The canal's role in facilitating international commerce is enormous, with billions of dollars worth of goods passing through each year. Yet, while the canal was initially built in the 19th century, its modern operation has evolved to meet the demands of contemporary maritime trade, incorporating advanced technologies, procedures, and infrastructure to ensure its efficient functioning in the 21st century.

One of the most critical aspects of how the Suez Canal works today lies in its capacity to accommodate a wide range of vessels, from container ships to oil tankers, bulk carriers, and cruise liners. Over the decades, the size of ships has grown significantly, with the development of mega vessels that can carry vast quantities of cargo. To keep up with this trend, the Suez Canal has undergone several expansions and modernization efforts. The most notable of these was the Suez Canal expansion project, completed in 2015, which added a new lane parallel to a 35-kilometer stretch of the canal. This expansion allows for two-way traffic, enabling ships to pass in opposite directions without needing to wait, a crucial improvement for reducing congestion and delays. The ability to accommodate ships with larger drafts (the depth of a ship's bottom from the waterline to the deepest point of the hull) has also been enhanced, making it possible for the canal to service larger vessels that would have previously struggled to navigate its waters.

The Suez Canal Authority (SCA), the Egyptian state-owned entity responsible for managing the canal, oversees the daily operation of this massive infrastructure. The authority is responsible for everything from setting tolls to maintaining the canal's infrastructure and ensuring the smooth passage of vessels. Ships traveling through the canal must pay a fee, known as a toll, which varies depending on the type of vessel, its size, and the cargo it is carrying. These tolls are a major source of revenue for Egypt, contributing significantly to the national economy. The amount of revenue generated by the canal has continued to grow as global trade increases, and as the canal expands its capacity, it is able to handle more traffic and thus generate even more income.

A critical component of the canal's operation today is the use of pilots, highly skilled mariners who guide ships through the waterway. Although the canal is relatively straightforward in its layout, stretching in a mostly straight line from north to south, navigating it is not without challenges. The canal is narrow, and ships must travel slowly to avoid causing damage to its banks or to other vessels. Additionally, ships must maintain precise positioning as they pass through, often within very tight margins. This is where pilots come in. Each ship that enters the Suez Canal is assigned a pilot who boards the vessel and takes over its navigation for the duration of the transit. These pilots are experts on the canal's unique conditions, including currents, weather patterns, and traffic flow, and they ensure that the ship passes through safely and efficiently.

The management of traffic within the canal is another essential aspect of its modern operation. The Suez Canal does not have locks, unlike other major canals like the Panama Canal, which means that ships are not stopped and lifted through different levels of water. Instead, the canal operates at sea level, which allows for continuous movement. However, due to the narrowness of the canal, there are specific points along its route where ships must stop and wait for others to pass. These are called "passing bays," where ships moving in one direction can wait while ships traveling in the opposite direction proceed through the main channel. With the expansion of the canal, the number of passing bays has been reduced, as ships can now transit more freely through the two-way sections. Still, traffic management is crucial to preventing bottlenecks and ensuring that ships move through the canal as smoothly as possible.

The canal operates 24 hours a day, with ships passing through in convoys. Typically, three convoys are organized each day—two traveling from the north (Port Said) to the south (Suez) and one traveling from the south to the north. Ships entering the canal join these convoys and follow strict schedules to ensure that traffic flows efficiently. Depending on the size and type of vessel, the passage through the canal can take anywhere from 11 to 16 hours, during which time the ship's crew works closely with the Suez Canal pilots and authorities to ensure a smooth transit. Despite the challenges of navigating the narrow waterway, the system of convoys and pilots ensures that traffic moves steadily and safely, with minimal delays.

The modernization of the Suez Canal has also incorporated advanced technologies to enhance safety and efficiency. One of the key technologies used today is the Vessel Traffic Management System (VTMS), a sophisticated radar and satellite-based monitoring system that tracks the movements of ships as they pass through the canal. The VTMS allows the Suez Canal Authority to monitor traffic in real-time, providing up-to-date information on the positions of vessels, weather conditions, and any potential hazards. This system helps to prevent collisions and other accidents, as well as ensuring that ships are adhering to their assigned schedules and routes. In the event of an emergency, such as a mechanical failure or a medical situation, the VTMS can alert authorities and dispatch assistance as needed.

In addition to technological advancements, the Suez Canal's infrastructure has been upgraded to meet the needs of modern maritime trade. The canal itself is regularly dredged to maintain its depth and ensure that it can accommodate larger ships. The banks of the canal are reinforced to prevent erosion, and navigational aids such as buoys and lights are constantly maintained and upgraded to guide ships through the canal safely, especially during night-time transits. The expansion project also included the construction of new bridges and tunnels to facilitate the movement of people and goods between the east and west sides of the canal, further enhancing its role as a key transportation hub.

The economic and geopolitical importance of the Suez Canal cannot be overstated. It remains one of the most important shipping routes in the world, with approximately 10% of global trade passing through its waters. For Egypt, the canal is not only a source of revenue but also a symbol of national pride and a critical asset in its economy. The canal's revenue helps fund infrastructure projects, social programs, and other national priorities, making it a vital part of the country's financial stability. Moreover, the canal's role in connecting Europe, Asia, and the Middle East makes it a key player in international politics and economics. Control over the canal has been a point of contention in the past, most notably during the Suez Crisis of 1956, and its strategic importance continues to influence Egypt's foreign policy and relationships with other nations.

The canal's role in global trade has also made it a focus of environmental and sustainability efforts. As concerns about climate change and pollution grow, the shipping industry is under increasing pressure to reduce its environmental impact. The Suez Canal Authority has responded to these concerns by implementing measures to reduce emissions from ships passing through the canal, such as encouraging the use of cleaner fuels and technologies. The authority has also taken steps to minimize the environmental impact of the canal itself, including efforts to protect the ecosystems of the Mediterranean and Red Seas from invasive species that may be introduced through the movement of ships.

In recent years, the Suez Canal has faced new challenges, particularly as global trade patterns shift and new competitors emerge. The rise of the Northern Sea Route, which allows ships to travel between Europe and Asia via the Arctic, poses a potential challenge to the canal's dominance. However, the Suez Canal remains the most reliable and cost-effective route for most ships, particularly those carrying oil, gas, and other bulk commodities. To remain competitive, the Suez Canal Authority continues to invest in upgrades and expansions, ensuring that the canal can handle the largest and most modern ships.

One of the most notable recent events involving the canal was the 2021 grounding of the container ship Ever Given, which blocked the canal for six days and caused significant disruption to global trade. The incident highlighted the vulnerability of the canal to accidents and underscored the importance of maintaining and upgrading its infrastructure to prevent such events in the future. In response to the Ever Given incident, the Suez Canal Authority has taken steps to improve safety, including enhancing the training of pilots, increasing the number of tugboats available for emergency assistance, and conducting additional dredging to widen and deepen key sections of the canal.

In conclusion, the Suez Canal operates today as a critical component of the global economy, facilitating the movement of goods between continents and playing a vital role in international trade. Its modern operation is a testament to the foresight of its creators and the ongoing efforts of the Suez Canal Authority to adapt the waterway to the needs of contemporary shipping. From the use of advanced technologies like the VTMS to the expansion of the canal's capacity and the implementation of environmental protections, the canal continues to evolve to meet the challenges of the 21st century. For the millions of people whose livelihoods depend on the canal, as well as for the nations and industries that rely on it for the movement of goods, the Suez Canal remains a vital and irreplaceable part of the global transportation network.

Chapter 14: The Canal's Environmental Impact

The environmental impact of the Suez Canal is a multifaceted issue that has been evolving ever since its construction. This waterway, which connects the Mediterranean Sea to the Red Sea, has played a crucial role in global trade, but it has also had significant ecological and environmental consequences. As the canal was initially constructed to serve economic and geopolitical interests, the potential for its environmental impact was not a major consideration at the time. However, in the modern era, the environmental consequences of this massive waterway have become more apparent and critical, affecting marine ecosystems, biodiversity, and even the climate. Understanding the environmental impact of the Suez Canal requires a deep dive into various aspects, including changes to marine life, the introduction of invasive species, pollution, and broader environmental concerns such as the canal's contribution to greenhouse gas emissions and climate change.

One of the most significant environmental impacts of the Suez Canal is its role as a corridor for the movement of marine species between the Mediterranean Sea and the Red Sea. Prior to the canal's construction, the Mediterranean and Red Seas were isolated from one another, each with its unique ecosystem. However, the opening of the canal created an artificial connection between these two bodies of water, allowing marine species from one region to migrate to the other. This process, known as "Lessepsian migration," named after the canal's architect Ferdinand de Lesseps, has had far-reaching consequences for the biodiversity of both seas. The Red Sea, which is part of the larger Indo-Pacific region, has a much richer and more diverse marine ecosystem compared to the Mediterranean. Many species from the Red Sea have taken advantage of the canal to colonize the Mediterranean, where they have often outcompeted native species, leading to significant shifts in the region's biodiversity.

Invasive species introduced through the Suez Canal have had a particularly profound impact on the Mediterranean's marine ecosystems. The arrival of species such as lionfish, jellyfish, and certain types of seaweed has disrupted local food chains, with some native species struggling to survive in the face of competition from these new arrivals. For instance, the rabbitfish, a species native to the Red Sea, has become one of the most invasive species in the Mediterranean, consuming vast amounts of seaweed and damaging habitats that are crucial for other marine life. The lionfish, another invasive species, is a voracious predator that has had a devastating impact on Mediterranean fish populations. These species have no natural predators in their new environment, allowing their populations to grow unchecked and leading to further ecological imbalances. The introduction of invasive species has also affected commercial fisheries in the Mediterranean, as some of the native species that are economically important, such as certain types of fish and shellfish, have declined in numbers due to competition from the invaders.

In addition to the movement of invasive species, the Suez Canal has also altered the physical and chemical properties of the water in both the Mediterranean and Red Seas. The Red Sea is more saline and warmer than the Mediterranean, and the exchange of water between the two seas through the canal has led to changes in salinity and temperature in parts of the Mediterranean, particularly in the eastern basin. These changes in water conditions have made the Mediterranean more hospitable to species from the Red Sea, further accelerating the process of Lessepsian migration. The altered water chemistry has also had an impact on native marine organisms, some of which are highly sensitive to changes in salinity and temperature. Coral reefs, in particular, have been affected by these shifts, with some species of

Mediterranean corals struggling to survive as the conditions in their habitats change.

Another major environmental concern associated with the Suez Canal is pollution. The canal is one of the busiest shipping routes in the world, with thousands of vessels passing through each year, many of them carrying hazardous cargo such as oil, chemicals, and other pollutants. The heavy traffic through the canal increases the risk of accidental spills and discharges of harmful substances into the water. Oil spills, in particular, are a major threat to marine life, as they can have devastating effects on ecosystems by smothering plants and animals, poisoning the water, and reducing oxygen levels. Even small amounts of oil can cause long-term damage to marine environments, and the potential for larger spills is always present given the volume of shipping traffic through the canal. In addition to oil, ships passing through the canal can discharge ballast water, which often contains harmful microorganisms, pathogens, and pollutants that can further degrade water quality and threaten marine life.

Noise pollution is another byproduct of the heavy shipping traffic in the canal. The noise generated by large ships can disturb marine animals, particularly those that rely on sound for communication and navigation, such as whales and dolphins. The constant noise from ship engines and propellers can interfere with the animals' ability to find food, locate mates, and avoid predators. In some cases, it can even cause physical harm, such as hearing loss or disorientation, leading to increased mortality rates among affected species. The impact of noise pollution on marine life is an area of growing concern, as the volume of shipping traffic through the canal continues to increase.

Beyond the immediate impacts on marine ecosystems, the Suez Canal also contributes to global environmental issues, particularly in relation to climate change. The shipping industry is a major source of greenhouse gas emissions, and the Suez Canal, as one of the world's busiest maritime routes, plays a role in the industry's carbon footprint.

Large container ships, oil tankers, and other vessels that pass through the canal burn significant amounts of fuel, releasing carbon dioxide (CO_2) and other pollutants into the atmosphere. While the canal itself reduces the overall distance that ships must travel between Europe and Asia, thereby cutting fuel consumption compared to longer alternative routes, the sheer volume of traffic still results in substantial emissions. In recent years, there has been growing pressure on the shipping industry to adopt cleaner technologies and reduce its environmental impact, but progress has been slow, and the Suez Canal remains a key link in a carbon-intensive global trade network.

In response to these environmental challenges, the Suez Canal Authority (SCA) has taken some steps to mitigate the canal's impact on the environment. One of the key initiatives has been the implementation of measures to control invasive species. For example, ships passing through the canal are required to follow strict ballast water management practices to reduce the risk of introducing non-native species into the Mediterranean. The SCA has also increased efforts to monitor and clean up pollution, including regular inspections of ships to ensure they comply with environmental regulations. Additionally, there are ongoing efforts to dredge and maintain the canal's waterway, not only to accommodate larger ships but also to minimize the environmental disruption caused by sediment buildup and erosion.

The canal's expansion in 2015, which included the construction of a new parallel lane, raised concerns about its potential environmental impact. While the expansion was aimed at increasing the canal's capacity and reducing congestion, environmental groups warned that it could lead to even greater biodiversity loss and exacerbate existing ecological problems. The expansion has allowed for more two-way traffic, which means that ships can pass through the canal more quickly and efficiently. However, this also increases the risk of further invasive species entering the Mediterranean, as the faster movement of ships through the canal may reduce the time available for measures like ballast water treatment to be effective.

One of the more indirect environmental impacts of the Suez Canal is its influence on global trade patterns and the associated environmental costs. By providing a faster and more efficient route between Europe and Asia, the canal has facilitated the growth of international shipping and global trade. While this has brought significant economic benefits, it has also contributed to the environmental costs associated with the production, transportation, and consumption of goods on a global scale. The environmental footprint of global trade includes not only the emissions from ships but also the deforestation, habitat destruction, and resource depletion that often result from the production of goods for export. The canal's role in enabling the expansion of global trade means that it is indirectly linked to these broader environmental challenges.

In the face of these environmental issues, there is growing recognition of the need for more sustainable practices in the operation of the Suez Canal and the shipping industry as a whole. International efforts to reduce greenhouse gas emissions, protect marine ecosystems, and promote cleaner technologies in shipping are critical to minimizing the environmental impact of this vital waterway. The shipping industry has begun exploring alternative fuels, such as liquefied natural gas (LNG) and hydrogen, as well as technologies like wind-assisted propulsion and electric engines, which could help reduce emissions from ships passing through the canal. However, the transition to greener shipping practices will take time, and the environmental challenges posed by the Suez Canal are likely to persist for the foreseeable future.

In conclusion, the Suez Canal's environmental impact is a complex and ongoing issue that spans a wide range of ecological and global concerns. From the introduction of invasive species to the pollution generated by heavy shipping traffic, the canal has had profound effects on marine ecosystems and biodiversity. At the same time, its role in global trade contributes to broader environmental challenges, including climate change and resource depletion. While efforts have been made to mitigate some of these impacts, the environmental consequences of the Suez Canal remain a pressing concern that requires continued attention and action from both the Suez Canal Authority and the global shipping industry. As the world grapples with the need for more sustainable practices, the future of the canal's operation will likely play a key role in shaping the environmental outcomes of international maritime trade.

Chapter 15: The Suez Canal's Economic Power

The Suez Canal stands as one of the most vital maritime arteries in the world, holding immense economic power and influence over global trade. Its strategic location, connecting the Mediterranean Sea with the Red Sea, provides a critical shortcut for ships traveling between Europe, Asia, and beyond. Without this man-made waterway, vessels would be forced to sail around the southern tip of Africa, adding weeks to their journeys and significantly increasing costs. The canal's significance cannot be overstated—it not only saves time and resources but also serves as a critical lifeline for the economies of nations that rely on maritime commerce. Since its opening in 1869, the Suez Canal has continually expanded in size, capacity, and importance, evolving from a colonial-era engineering marvel into a central pillar of global trade and economic development. Its economic power is tied to its role as a gateway for commerce, the revenues it generates, its effect on oil and energy markets, its geopolitical significance, and the impact it has on the economies of countries that benefit from its operations.

One of the canal's most obvious and immediate economic impacts comes from the way it reduces shipping time and costs for vessels moving between Europe and Asia. By cutting approximately 7,000 kilometers off the alternative route around the Cape of Good Hope, the Suez Canal offers a massive reduction in transportation time—saving up to 10 to 12 days depending on the ship's speed. This reduction in travel time means a corresponding reduction in fuel costs, labor costs, and wear and tear on ships, all of which make the canal route far more economically viable. Shipping companies can carry goods faster, meet demand more efficiently, and reduce operating expenses, which has ripple effects across the global economy. This is especially important for industries that rely on just-in-time production and delivery systems, such as electronics, automotive, and textiles, where delays in shipping can lead to costly disruptions in production and distribution.

The canal's ability to accommodate vessels of all kinds—from container ships and bulk carriers to tankers transporting oil and liquefied natural gas (LNG)—further enhances its economic influence. Each year, approximately 18,000 to 20,000 vessels transit the Suez Canal, carrying a wide variety of goods, raw materials, and commodities. These goods range from consumer products, like electronics and clothing, to essential resources, such as crude oil, LNG, and agricultural products. In this context, the canal is not just a passageway for ships but a conduit for the global flow of goods that underpin modern economies. The Suez Canal thus plays a key role in keeping international trade routes flowing smoothly, and any disruption in its operations has immediate and far-reaching consequences for businesses and economies around the world.

Perhaps one of the most critical sectors affected by the Suez Canal is the global oil and energy market. A significant portion of the world's oil supply passes through the canal, making it an essential link in the global energy chain. Roughly 8-10% of the world's seaborne oil trade, including oil from the Middle East destined for Europe and North America, passes through the Suez Canal. In addition to crude oil, the canal is also a major route for LNG exports, particularly from Qatar, one of the world's leading suppliers of natural gas. The canal's role in the transportation of energy products gives it considerable leverage over the global energy market. A blockage or disruption of traffic through the canal, as seen in the 2021 incident involving the container ship Ever Given, can send shockwaves through global oil prices and energy supply chains. Any interruption in the canal's operation typically leads to a spike in oil prices, as companies scramble to find alternative routes or delay deliveries. This, in turn, impacts fuel costs and has cascading effects on other industries reliant on oil, such as manufacturing, transportation, and logistics.

The revenues generated by the Suez Canal are a key driver of economic power, both for Egypt and the broader global economy. The Suez Canal Authority (SCA), which manages the waterway, collects tolls from ships passing through the canal, and these tolls are a major source of revenue for the Egyptian government. The canal is one of Egypt's largest sources of foreign currency earnings, alongside tourism, remittances from Egyptians working abroad, and natural gas exports. In recent years, annual revenue from the Suez Canal has ranged between $5 and $6 billion, making it an essential contributor to the national economy. This revenue is used to fund public services, infrastructure projects, and social programs, providing a lifeline for the Egyptian economy, which has faced challenges such as political instability, economic downturns, and the COVID-19 pandemic. The expansion of the canal in 2015, which added a second lane and allowed for two-way traffic, has only increased its revenue-generating potential, as it can now accommodate larger ships and more traffic, further enhancing its economic importance.

The toll fees collected by the SCA are structured according to the type of vessel, its size, and its cargo. For instance, oil tankers and container ships typically pay higher tolls than smaller vessels or bulk carriers, reflecting the higher value of their cargo and the economic importance of their transit. The fees can run into the hundreds of thousands of dollars per ship, and given the number of vessels that pass through the canal each day, these tolls add up to significant revenue. For shipping companies, paying the toll is still far more economical than the alternative of taking the longer route around the Cape of Good Hope, which would incur higher fuel and operating costs. As a result, the Suez Canal's toll structure gives it considerable economic power, as it remains a highly attractive option for ships despite the relatively high cost of transit.

The geopolitical significance of the Suez Canal also adds to its economic power. Throughout its history, control of the canal has been a point of contention between world powers. The canal is not just an economic asset but a strategic one, serving as a vital link between Europe, Asia, and the Middle East. Whoever controls the canal has the ability to influence global trade routes and, by extension, the global economy. This was particularly evident during the Suez Crisis of 1956 when Egyptian President Gamal Abdel Nasser nationalized the canal, prompting a military intervention by Britain, France, and Israel. The crisis highlighted the strategic importance of the canal, as it controls access to key shipping routes for oil and other goods. In the modern era, the canal remains a geopolitical asset, and its security and stability are of paramount concern to global powers. This strategic importance gives Egypt leverage in international affairs, as control of the canal provides a measure of influence over global trade and the economies of countries that rely on the canal for their imports and exports.

Another aspect of the canal's economic power is its role in the globalization of supply chains. The canal has facilitated the movement of goods between distant regions of the world, helping to integrate economies and foster international trade. By making it easier and more cost-effective to transport goods across the globe, the canal has contributed to the rise of global supply chains, where products are manufactured in multiple countries and assembled in others. For example, raw materials might be sourced from Africa, components manufactured in Asia, and final products assembled in Europe, with the Suez Canal providing the critical link that allows for the seamless movement of goods between these regions. This interconnectedness has allowed companies to take advantage of cost savings and efficiencies, further driving economic growth and development. The canal has, in essence, become a symbol of the globalized economy, where goods and services are exchanged across borders on an unprecedented scale.

The expansion of the canal in 2015 further cemented its economic importance by allowing it to handle even larger ships, known as Ultra-Large Container Ships (ULCS), which can carry up to 20,000 twenty-foot equivalent units (TEUs). The ability to accommodate these massive vessels has made the canal more competitive and attractive to shipping companies, as they can now transport larger volumes of goods in a single trip. This has led to increased traffic through the canal and higher revenue for the SCA, while also benefiting global supply chains by reducing shipping costs per unit of cargo. The expansion has also reduced congestion, allowing ships to pass through the canal more quickly and efficiently, further enhancing its role as a critical economic artery.

In addition to its impact on global trade, the canal also plays a role in the regional economy. Cities and towns along the canal's route, such as Port Said, Ismailia, and Suez, benefit from the economic activity generated by the canal. These cities have become hubs of commerce, industry, and logistics, providing services to ships passing through the canal and to the workers who maintain and operate it. The canal also supports a wide range of industries, including shipbuilding, repair, and maintenance, as well as tourism, as visitors come to see the canal and learn about its history. The expansion of the canal has further stimulated economic development in the region, creating jobs and boosting local economies.

In conclusion, the Suez Canal's economic power is vast and multifaceted. It plays a central role in global trade, facilitating the movement of goods between Europe, Asia, and beyond, while significantly reducing shipping time and costs. Its impact on the oil and energy markets, its role in the globalization of supply chains, and its contribution to the Egyptian economy through toll revenues all highlight its economic importance. The canal's geopolitical significance and its role in regional development further underscore its influence. As the world's economies become increasingly interconnected, the Suez Canal will continue to be a vital link in the global trade network, shaping the flow of commerce and contributing to economic growth for decades to come.

Chapter 16: Famous Ships of the Suez Canal

The *Suez Canal* has played a pivotal role in the journeys of countless ships over its long and storied history, many of which have gone on to become famous or historically significant due to their size, cargo, or the events that transpired during their passage. These ships represent a variety of purposes—some were milestones of engineering, others carried goods of global importance, while others found themselves at the center of major geopolitical incidents. The canal's fame as one of the world's most important waterways is deeply intertwined with the stories of the ships that have traversed its length, each leaving a unique mark on its history. From luxurious ocean liners to colossal tankers, from cargo vessels carrying vital goods to ships embroiled in wars and blockades, the Suez Canal has seen them all.

One of the most iconic ships to have passed through the Suez Canal is the SS *United States*, the American ocean liner that, during its heyday, was a symbol of luxury, speed, and national pride. Built in the early 1950s, the *United States* was designed to be the fastest ocean liner in the world, and it held the Blue Riband—the prize awarded for the fastest transatlantic crossing—for many years. While its usual route was across the Atlantic between New York and Europe, the ship did pass through the Suez Canal on special voyages, showcasing American maritime prowess in an era when international travel was dominated by ocean liners. The *United States* represented a combination of speed, luxury, and cutting-edge engineering, and its journey through the Suez Canal marked a union between two icons of global transportation—the world's fastest ocean liner and the world's most important waterway.

Another notable vessel associated with the Suez Canal is the SS *France*, one of the largest and most luxurious ocean liners ever built.

The *France*, launched in 1960, was known for its grandeur and elegance, representing the height of French engineering and design. Though primarily used for transatlantic crossings between France and the United States, the ship also made its way through the Suez Canal on special cruises, drawing international attention to both the ship and the canal. The passage of such large, celebrated liners through the canal demonstrated the global importance of the waterway, as even ships designed for other regions found themselves using the canal for special journeys, highlighting its role in facilitating luxury cruises and showcasing European maritime achievements.

In addition to luxurious ocean liners, the Suez Canal has been the stage for vessels that played crucial roles in international trade and energy markets. One such ship was the *Knock Nevis*, a supertanker that holds the title of the largest ship ever built. The *Knock Nevis* was so massive that it could not transit the Suez Canal in its fully loaded state, due to the canal's size limitations at the time. However, its presence in the vicinity of the canal is significant because it represents the kind of vessels that forced changes in the canal's infrastructure. In the years following the construction of the *Knock Nevis* and other similarly large tankers, the canal underwent several expansions to accommodate larger and heavier ships, underscoring the importance of keeping the canal up to date with the evolving needs of global trade. The sheer size and scale of the *Knock Nevis*—a floating behemoth over 1,500 feet long and capable of carrying more than half a million tons of crude oil—illustrate the challenges and opportunities that large ships present to the Suez Canal, and how such vessels have shaped the future of the waterway.

Oil tankers, in particular, have had a long association with the Suez Canal, given its vital role as a transit point for crude oil and petroleum products traveling from the Middle East to Europe and North America. One famous tanker was the *MT Haven*, an oil tanker that tragically sank off the coast of Italy in 1991 after an explosion.

Though the ship did not sink in the Suez Canal itself, it had frequently used the canal during its voyages, and the disaster was a reminder of the risks associated with the transportation of oil, especially through such important waterways. The sinking of the *Haven* resulted in one of the largest oil spills in history, with lasting environmental consequences, and served as a wake-up call to the global shipping industry regarding the dangers of transporting hazardous materials through narrow and heavily trafficked waterways like the Suez Canal.

Beyond the commercial and luxury ships, the Suez Canal has also seen its share of military vessels, many of which have become famous for their roles in conflicts or geopolitical events. One of the most notable examples is the passage of British and French warships during the Suez Crisis of 1956. In response to Egyptian President Gamal Abdel Nasser's nationalization of the canal, Britain, France, and Israel launched a military intervention aimed at regaining control of the waterway. British and French warships passed through the Mediterranean and into the canal zone, where they attempted to seize key positions. The crisis not only underscored the importance of the canal as a strategic asset but also brought the role of military vessels in the canal's history into sharp focus. These warships symbolized the intersection of global politics, military power, and the vital economic and strategic significance of the canal, making the Suez Crisis one of the most famous episodes in the canal's history.

In more recent times, one of the most famous ships to transit the Suez Canal is the container ship *Ever Given*. In March 2021, the *Ever Given* became lodged in the canal, blocking all traffic for six days and causing a global shipping crisis. The ship, one of the largest container vessels in the world, became wedged across the canal after strong winds pushed it off course, leading to one of the most infamous maritime incidents in modern history. The blockage of the Suez Canal by the *Ever Given* had immediate and severe economic consequences, as hundreds of ships were delayed, and global supply chains were disrupted. The incident highlighted the vulnerability of the canal and the global economy to such disruptions, as well as the increasing size of modern ships and the challenges they pose to the safe and efficient operation of the canal. The *Ever Given* became a household name overnight, symbolizing both the scale of modern maritime commerce and the fragility of global trade networks.

The *Ever Given* incident was a reminder that the Suez Canal, despite its advanced infrastructure and strategic importance, remains susceptible to accidents and blockages, particularly as the size of ships continues to increase. The canal's expansion in 2015, which added a new lane to allow for two-way traffic in certain sections, was intended to reduce congestion and improve safety, but the sheer size of vessels like the *Ever Given* presents new challenges for the waterway. The incident also underscored the critical importance of the canal in global trade, as even a brief blockage had ripple effects across industries ranging from electronics and automobiles to food and energy.

In addition to the ships mentioned above, many other vessels have contributed to the Suez Canal's rich history. Passenger liners, cargo ships, military vessels, and oil tankers have all played their part in making the canal the vital waterway it is today. Each ship that passes through the canal is part of a much larger story, one that encompasses global trade, international relations, technological advancement, and economic development. From the early days of steam-powered ships navigating the newly opened canal to the modern era of ultra-large container vessels and supertankers, the Suez Canal has remained at the heart of global maritime activity, and the ships that use it are a testament to the canal's enduring significance.

As the canal continues to evolve, accommodating larger ships and higher volumes of traffic, new vessels will undoubtedly make their mark on its history. The expansion projects, technological advancements in shipbuilding, and the ongoing importance of the canal to global commerce mean that future ships will continue to write new chapters in the story of the Suez Canal. Whether they are luxury liners, massive tankers, or innovative cargo vessels, these ships will further cement the canal's place as one of the most important and famous waterways in the world. Each ship, in its own way, contributes to the legacy of the canal, and their stories are intertwined with the history of one of the world's greatest engineering feats.

Chapter 17: The Canal in Modern Politics

The Suez Canal, since its completion in the mid-19th century, has always been more than just a vital trade route. It has been a geopolitical flashpoint, an economic powerhouse, and a symbol of national sovereignty and global power dynamics. In modern politics, the canal continues to wield significant influence over global trade, diplomacy, and military strategy. The canal's location—connecting the Mediterranean Sea to the Red Sea, and thus linking Europe, Asia, and Africa—places it at the heart of international political and economic calculations. Over the decades, its role in modern politics has evolved in response to shifting power structures, regional conflicts, global trade demands, and environmental challenges. Today, the Suez Canal remains as politically charged as ever, and the various countries and interests surrounding it continue to navigate a complex web of competing priorities.

One of the most significant political aspects of the Suez Canal today is its role in Egypt's economy and national identity. The canal is one of Egypt's most important sources of revenue, generating billions of dollars annually from the tolls collected from ships transiting the waterway. The canal's significance to Egypt's economy means that the Egyptian government, led by President Abdel Fattah el-Sisi, has placed great emphasis on maintaining and expanding the canal to ensure its continued profitability. In 2015, Egypt completed an ambitious project to widen and deepen the canal, allowing for larger ships and increased traffic. This expansion was seen as a demonstration of Egypt's ability to modernize its infrastructure and maintain its status as a crucial player in global trade. Politically, the canal's expansion bolstered President el-Sisi's image as a leader capable of delivering large-scale economic projects, while also reaffirming Egypt's sovereignty over the canal—a critical issue since the nationalization of the waterway in 1956.

The canal's importance to Egypt's economy is also tied to its broader political role in the region. For Egypt, control of the canal represents more than just economic power; it symbolizes the country's strategic influence in the Middle East and North Africa. In a region marked by political instability, conflicts, and shifting alliances, the Suez Canal remains one of the few constants in Egypt's political landscape. The country's ability to control access to such a vital artery of global trade gives it leverage in international relations, especially with major powers like the United States, China, and the European Union, which rely on the canal for the smooth flow of goods and energy resources. This leverage allows Egypt to position itself as a key mediator and player in regional politics, whether in peace negotiations, economic cooperation, or military partnerships.

However, the canal's geopolitical importance also makes it a potential target for conflict and tension. Historically, the canal has been the site of several military confrontations, most notably the Suez Crisis of 1956, when Egypt's nationalization of the canal led to a military intervention by Britain, France, and Israel. While that specific crisis was resolved, the canal has remained vulnerable to regional instability, particularly during periods of war or political upheaval. In recent years, concerns about the security of the canal have resurfaced due to the ongoing unrest in the Middle East, including conflicts in Yemen, Syria, and Libya, as well as tensions between regional powers like Iran and Saudi Arabia. For Egypt, maintaining control and security over the canal is a top priority, as any disruption to the waterway could have devastating economic consequences for the country, as well as global ramifications for trade.

In addition to regional instability, the canal also plays a role in broader international political and economic rivalries. One of the most significant modern political dynamics involving the canal is the competition between the United States and China for influence in global trade and geopolitics. As the world's two largest economies, both the U.S. and China have a vested interest in ensuring the smooth flow of goods through the Suez Canal. For China, the canal is a critical link in its Belt and Road Initiative (BRI), a massive infrastructure and investment project aimed at enhancing trade routes between Asia, Europe, and Africa. Chinese companies have invested heavily in ports and infrastructure projects along the BRI, including in countries near the Suez Canal, such as Egypt and Djibouti. These investments are part of China's broader strategy to secure its supply chains and enhance its influence in key regions.

For the United States, the Suez Canal represents not only an important trade route but also a key component of its military strategy in the Middle East. The U.S. Navy regularly uses the canal to move warships between the Mediterranean and the Indian Ocean, allowing for rapid deployment in times of crisis. This military presence underscores the canal's strategic value, not just for trade, but for the projection of power. The U.S. also has a strong interest in maintaining stability in the region, as any conflict or disruption to the canal could have far-reaching consequences for global energy markets and U.S. allies in Europe and Asia. The U.S. and its NATO allies rely on the canal for the transport of oil and gas from the Middle East, and any blockage of the canal could lead to significant disruptions in energy supplies.

The Suez Canal's importance to global energy markets cannot be overstated. A significant portion of the world's oil and liquefied natural gas (LNG) passes through the canal, making it a critical chokepoint for the global energy industry. Countries like Saudi Arabia, the United Arab Emirates, and Qatar export vast quantities of oil and gas through the canal to Europe and North America. As a result, any political or military developments in the region that affect the canal's operation can have an immediate impact on global energy prices. For example, the 2021 blockage of the canal by the *Ever Given* container ship led to temporary spikes in oil prices and widespread concerns about supply chain disruptions. This incident highlighted the canal's continued vulnerability to both natural and man-made disasters, as well as its central role in global energy politics.

Another aspect of the canal's modern political significance is its role in environmental and climate-related issues. As the world grapples with the challenges of climate change, the Suez Canal has become a focal point for discussions about the environmental impact of global shipping. The canal allows ships to take a shorter route between Europe and Asia, reducing fuel consumption and greenhouse gas emissions compared to alternative routes like the Cape of Good Hope. However, the increased traffic through the canal also raises concerns about pollution, invasive species, and the impact of dredging and construction on local ecosystems. Environmental groups have called for greater oversight and regulation of shipping through the canal to minimize its environmental footprint, while also recognizing the canal's importance in reducing the overall carbon emissions of global trade.

In the context of international diplomacy, the canal is often a subject of negotiations and agreements between Egypt and other countries. Egypt has used the canal as a bargaining chip in its relations with neighboring countries and global powers, offering preferential treatment or discounted tolls to countries that align with its political and economic interests. At the same time, Egypt has sought to maintain its sovereignty over the canal and resist outside pressure to cede control or management of the waterway. The canal has also been a topic of discussion in regional organizations like the Arab League and the African Union, as Egypt seeks to balance its national interests with the broader goals of regional cooperation and development.

The canal's strategic importance has also led to increased interest from other global powers, such as Russia and India, both of which have sought to strengthen their ties with Egypt and secure access to the canal for their shipping and military needs. Russia, in particular, has been expanding its influence in the Middle East and North Africa in recent years, and the Suez Canal is seen as a key element of its strategy to project power in the region. India, too, views the canal as critical to its growing trade relationships with Europe and Africa, and has worked to deepen its diplomatic and economic ties with Egypt.

In conclusion, the Suez Canal remains a central player in modern politics, serving as a crucial link in global trade, a strategic asset in military and geopolitical calculations, and a symbol of national sovereignty for Egypt. Its role in regional and international politics is shaped by a complex web of economic, environmental, and security considerations, making it one of the most important and politically charged waterways in the world. As global trade continues to grow, and as political and environmental challenges evolve, the Suez Canal will remain a key focal point for international diplomacy, economic development, and geopolitical strategy for many years to come.

Chapter 18: Navigating the Suez Canal

Navigating the Suez Canal is an intricate and highly regulated process that reflects both the historical significance and modern-day importance of this vital waterway. Stretching approximately 120 miles from Port Said on the Mediterranean Sea to Suez on the Red Sea, the canal is an essential conduit for global maritime traffic, allowing vessels to bypass the lengthy journey around the southern tip of Africa. The canal is not just a simple waterway; it is a highly engineered and carefully controlled environment where ships from all over the world pass through a narrow, human-made channel under stringent guidelines, navigational rules, and precise coordination to ensure smooth passage. The navigation of the Suez Canal today involves numerous technologies, protocols, and human expertise that work together to manage one of the most crucial maritime routes on the planet.

The process of navigating the canal begins long before a ship arrives at its entrance. Due to the narrowness of the canal and the constant traffic in both directions, ships must be carefully scheduled in convoys to avoid congestion and ensure safe passage. Ships intending to navigate the canal must register their passage in advance and adhere to strict timetables set by the Suez Canal Authority (SCA), which manages and oversees all operations. The canal is open 24 hours a day, but ships are arranged into convoys that usually depart in the early morning and evening. This scheduling allows for an orderly and efficient flow of traffic, with some convoys passing northbound from the Red Sea to the Mediterranean, while others move southbound in the opposite direction. The convoy system is essential, as the canal is a single-lane passage for most of its length, although there are certain stretches, like the Great Bitter Lake, where ships can pass one another.

Once a ship arrives at one of the canal's entrances, either at Port Said in the north or Suez in the south, the vessel must undergo rigorous checks and inspections. These checks include a review of the ship's paperwork, cargo, and compliance with international maritime regulations. The Suez Canal Authority imposes strict guidelines for ships navigating the canal, including specific safety protocols, environmental regulations, and the size of the vessel. The canal has a maximum allowable draft, which is the depth of the ship's hull below the waterline, and only ships that meet these size and safety requirements are permitted to enter. The increasing size of modern ships has posed challenges to navigation, and this has led to significant expansions and deepening projects to accommodate larger vessels. Even with these improvements, many of the world's largest ships, including supertankers and mega-container ships, must be specially designed to fit within the canal's parameters.

Before entering the canal, ships are also required to take on board an official Suez Canal pilot. Pilots are highly trained mariners employed by the SCA who are experts in navigating the canal's unique waters. These pilots take command of the ship for the duration of its passage through the canal, guiding it through the various bends, currents, and narrow stretches. The pilot's knowledge of the canal's depth, tides, and navigational hazards is essential for the safe transit of ships, particularly for those that are heavily laden or of considerable size. While the ship's captain remains responsible for the overall safety and operation of the vessel, the pilot's intimate familiarity with the canal ensures that the passage is as smooth and safe as possible. The pilot boards the ship at either Port Said or Suez and remains on board throughout the entire transit, which can take anywhere from 12 to 16 hours, depending on the ship's speed and the convoy's movement.

Navigating the Suez Canal requires a delicate balance of speed, precision, and coordination. Ships are generally limited to a maximum speed of about 8 to 10 knots (approximately 15 to 18 kilometers per hour) to reduce the risk of accidents and minimize the impact on the canal's banks and surrounding environment. The canal's width, particularly in its narrower stretches, allows little room for error, and the slow speed ensures that ships have adequate time to make adjustments to their course if necessary. Moreover, the slow speed helps prevent the wash—the waves generated by a ship's movement—from eroding the banks of the canal. As ships navigate the canal, they pass through several different zones, including stretches of open water, where the canal widens, as well as narrower passages that require precise steering to avoid running aground.

One of the most significant challenges in navigating the Suez Canal is the variability of the canal's depth and width. Although the canal has been deepened and widened in recent years to accommodate larger vessels, certain sections remain narrow and shallow, making navigation particularly tricky for large ships. These ships often have to reduce their draft—essentially the depth to which they sit in the water—by offloading some cargo or reducing ballast before entering the canal. Once inside, the depth of the canal fluctuates slightly due to factors like tidal movements and sedimentation, which can create unexpected challenges. To mitigate these risks, the Suez Canal Authority has installed advanced navigational aids, including buoys, radar systems, and GPS tracking, to help guide ships along their route. These systems work in tandem with the canal pilots to ensure that ships stay on course and avoid potential hazards.

In addition to natural challenges, ships navigating the canal must also contend with the sheer volume of traffic passing through the waterway. On any given day, more than 50 ships may transit the canal, carrying everything from consumer goods and industrial machinery to oil and gas. The density of traffic means that ships must maintain strict adherence to their designated positions within the convoy and communicate constantly with other vessels and the canal authorities. Ships must also be prepared to stop or slow down at a moment's notice if there is a delay further up the canal or if a ship ahead encounters difficulty. Communication between the ships, pilots, and Suez Canal

Authority is constant throughout the transit, with every movement carefully monitored and coordinated.

The passage through the canal is not entirely uninterrupted. At various points along the canal, ships pass through waiting areas or larger bodies of water, like the Great Bitter Lake, where ships can anchor if needed. These pauses allow for the organization of convoys, repairs, or even crew changes. The Great Bitter Lake, located roughly halfway along the canal, is a particularly important feature of the waterway as it allows ships to anchor safely while waiting for convoys to pass or for clearance to continue. This section of the canal is wide enough to accommodate large vessels and serves as a temporary holding area, preventing congestion and ensuring a smooth flow of traffic.

One of the most crucial aspects of navigating the Suez Canal is ensuring compliance with the environmental regulations imposed by the Suez Canal Authority. Ships passing through the canal must adhere to strict pollution control measures, including the disposal of waste, the prevention of oil spills, and the use of environmentally friendly ballast water management systems. The canal passes through environmentally sensitive areas, and any pollution or disruption to the ecosystem could have long-term consequences for the region. The SCA has implemented measures to monitor water quality and ensure that ships comply with international environmental standards, including the International Maritime Organization's (IMO) regulations on emissions and waste disposal. Ships that violate these regulations can face significant fines or be denied passage through the canal.

The passage through the canal culminates as ships approach either the northern or southern exit, depending on their direction of travel. In the north, ships enter the Mediterranean Sea via Port Said, while in the south, they exit into the Red Sea at the city of Suez. Before leaving the canal, ships must complete one final inspection to ensure that they have met all regulatory and safety requirements. Once cleared, the canal pilot disembarks, and the ship is free to continue its journey. For the thousands of ships that pass through the canal each year, the successful navigation of this narrow, congested, and highly regulated waterway represents a critical achievement in global maritime logistics.

The importance of smooth navigation through the Suez Canal cannot be overstated. As one of the world's busiest maritime corridors, the canal plays a pivotal role in the global supply chain, with millions of tons of cargo passing through it each year. Disruptions to canal traffic, such as accidents or blockages, can have widespread repercussions for international trade and energy markets. This was demonstrated in March 2021, when the *Ever Given*, one of the world's largest container ships, ran aground and blocked the canal for six days. The blockage caused a significant backlog of ships, delayed billions of dollars' worth of goods, and highlighted the vulnerability of the global supply chain to disruptions in this critical waterway.

In conclusion, navigating the Suez Canal is a complex and highly coordinated process that involves careful planning, precise navigation, and strict adherence to regulations. The canal's narrow and shallow waters, combined with the high volume of traffic and environmental sensitivities, make it one of the most challenging maritime routes in the world. Despite these challenges, the canal remains a vital artery for global trade, facilitating the movement of goods between Europe, Asia, and Africa and playing a crucial role in the global economy.

Chapter 19: The Canal in the Digital Age

In the digital age, the Suez Canal has undergone a significant transformation, as technological advancements have reshaped how this vital waterway is managed, navigated, and integrated into the broader global economy. The canal, long a symbol of international trade and maritime power, now operates with the assistance of cutting-edge digital tools that enhance safety, efficiency, and environmental responsibility. The increasing complexity of global trade, the rising demands of shipping logistics, and the growing size of modern vessels have made the integration of digital technologies not only beneficial but essential to the functioning of the canal. From real-time monitoring systems and automation to big data analytics and artificial intelligence, the Suez Canal has embraced the digital era in a manner that keeps it at the forefront of global maritime routes, ensuring its relevance in the 21st century.

One of the most profound impacts of the digital age on the Suez Canal has been the implementation of sophisticated navigation systems. Modern ships, many of which are larger and more technologically advanced than ever, require precise guidance through the narrow and congested canal. Traditional methods of navigation, while still relevant, are now supplemented by high-tech systems such as Global Positioning System (GPS) technology, advanced radar, and satellite tracking. Ships navigating the canal are equipped with GPS systems that provide real-time data on their exact location, speed, and trajectory. This information is crucial, given the canal's narrowness and the limited room for error, especially for massive vessels like supertankers and mega-container ships. The use of GPS has minimized the risk of accidents, such as running aground, and has made it easier for ships to stay within the designated shipping lanes.

Digital mapping and geographic information system (GIS) technology have also become indispensable for the operation of the

Suez Canal. The canal's depth, width, and underwater topography are constantly monitored and mapped using digital tools, ensuring that ships are aware of any potential hazards along the route. These digital maps are updated in real-time and provide precise data on tides, currents, and weather conditions, all of which can influence a ship's passage through the canal. The integration of these systems with the existing navigational aids has significantly reduced the risk of human error and improved overall safety. Moreover, the Suez Canal Authority (SCA) uses this technology to provide ship captains and pilots with accurate information about water levels and conditions, enabling them to make informed decisions during their journey.

In the digital age, the role of the Suez Canal pilots has also evolved. While the canal still requires a physical pilot to board each ship and guide it through the waterway, these pilots are now equipped with state-of-the-art digital tools to assist in their work. Pilots use handheld devices and tablets loaded with specialized software that provides up-to-the-minute information on the ship's location, speed, and the conditions in the canal. This digital assistance allows pilots to make real-time adjustments to a ship's course, ensuring smoother navigation through the canal's narrow stretches. These devices also enable communication between the pilot, the ship's captain, and the canal's control centers, allowing for better coordination and quicker responses to any issues that may arise. The integration of digital technology into the work of the pilots has significantly improved the efficiency and safety of canal navigation.

Another critical aspect of the Suez Canal's digital transformation is the implementation of real-time monitoring systems. The canal is equipped with an extensive network of sensors, cameras, and radar systems that constantly monitor the movement of ships, environmental conditions, and other factors that could impact navigation. This digital infrastructure allows the Suez Canal Authority to track every ship passing through the canal in real time, ensuring that all vessels are following the correct protocols and maintaining safe distances from one another. The ability to monitor the entire canal from centralized control rooms has reduced the likelihood of accidents and has made it easier to manage the heavy traffic that the canal regularly experiences. In the event of an emergency, these systems allow the canal's authorities to respond quickly and efficiently, minimizing disruption to the flow of traffic.

The canal's control centers, which are now outfitted with digital dashboards and monitoring systems, play a crucial role in managing the day-to-day operations of the waterway. These control centers use artificial intelligence (AI) and machine learning algorithms to analyze the vast amounts of data generated by the canal's sensors and monitoring systems. The AI systems can predict potential bottlenecks, identify ships that may require special attention, and optimize the scheduling of convoys to ensure a smooth and efficient flow of traffic. This data-driven approach has revolutionized the management of the canal, allowing for more precise decision-making and improving the overall efficiency of the canal's operations. The use of AI and machine learning also helps the canal's authorities to anticipate maintenance needs, predict changes in traffic patterns, and adjust their strategies accordingly.

Big data analytics is another key component of the canal's digital transformation. Every ship that passes through the canal generates a wealth of data, including information about its cargo, destination, speed, and fuel consumption. This data is collected and analyzed by the Suez Canal Authority to gain insights into global shipping trends, the efficiency of the canal, and the environmental impact of its operations. By analyzing this data, the SCA can make informed decisions about future investments in the canal's infrastructure, such as deepening certain sections or expanding the canal to accommodate larger ships. Big data analytics also allows the SCA to optimize the scheduling of convoys, reducing wait times for ships and ensuring that the canal operates at maximum capacity.

The digital age has also brought about significant changes in how the Suez Canal handles financial transactions. In the past, ships navigating the canal had to deal with time-consuming paperwork and payment processes. Today, much of this has been streamlined through digital platforms that allow for faster and more efficient transactions. Ships can now submit their documentation electronically, pay tolls online, and receive immediate confirmation of their passage through the canal. The digitalization of these processes has reduced the administrative burden on both the ships and the canal's authorities, freeing up resources that can be used to improve the overall operation of the canal. Additionally, the use of blockchain technology is being explored as a way to further enhance the security and transparency of financial transactions related to the canal.

In the context of environmental management, the digital age has introduced new tools for monitoring and mitigating the environmental impact of the Suez Canal. The canal passes through ecologically sensitive areas, and the Suez Canal Authority has implemented a range of digital technologies to ensure that ships passing through the canal comply with international environmental regulations. Ships are now required to use ballast water management systems that prevent the spread of invasive species, and digital sensors monitor the water quality in the canal to detect any potential pollution. The SCA has also adopted emissions monitoring technologies to ensure that ships adhere to international standards for reducing greenhouse gas emissions. The canal's environmental monitoring systems are integrated with the global environmental reporting networks, allowing for real-time tracking of the canal's ecological impact.

As part of its efforts to further modernize the canal, the Suez Canal Authority has also embraced the use of automation and autonomous shipping technologies. While fully autonomous ships are still in the early stages of development, the canal is preparing for a future where ships equipped with autonomous navigation systems may regularly pass through its waters. To accommodate these advancements, the SCA is investing in the development of digital infrastructure that can communicate with autonomous ships, ensuring that they can navigate the canal safely and efficiently. This includes the development of smart buoys, automated control systems, and digital communication networks that will enable real-time interaction between autonomous ships and the canal's control centers. The SCA is also working with international maritime organizations to develop standards and regulations for the safe operation of autonomous ships in the canal.

The integration of digital technologies into the operation of the Suez Canal has also had a significant impact on global supply chain management. The ability to track ships in real-time, predict arrival times, and monitor the status of cargo has made it easier for shipping companies and logistics providers to plan their operations. This level of transparency and visibility has reduced the risk of delays and disruptions, allowing for more efficient coordination between ships, ports, and land-based transportation networks. Digital platforms now enable shipping companies to manage their entire supply chains from a single interface, with real-time updates on the status of their vessels and cargo as they pass through the canal. This level of connectivity has revolutionized global trade, making the movement of goods faster, more predictable, and more cost-effective.

In conclusion, the digital age has brought about a profound transformation in how the Suez Canal operates. The integration of advanced technologies such as GPS, AI, big data analytics, and real-time monitoring systems has made the canal safer, more efficient, and more environmentally responsible. These digital tools have revolutionized the management of the canal, allowing for better coordination of ship traffic, more precise navigation, and faster financial transactions. As the world continues to embrace digitalization, the Suez Canal remains at the cutting edge of technological innovation, ensuring that it will continue to play a pivotal role in global trade for years to come. With ongoing investments in digital infrastructure, the canal is well-positioned to meet the challenges of the 21st century and beyond, maintaining its status as one of the most important maritime routes in the world.

Chapter 20: The Future of the Suez Canal

The future of the Suez Canal is shaped by a combination of emerging technological advancements, shifting global trade patterns, environmental concerns, and geopolitical developments. As one of the world's most crucial waterways, the Suez Canal has long played a pivotal role in global commerce by facilitating the movement of goods between Europe, Asia, and Africa. However, as the 21st century unfolds, the canal faces both new challenges and unprecedented opportunities. With its historical significance as a vital artery for international trade, the Suez Canal must evolve to meet the demands of a rapidly changing world. The future of the canal is likely to be marked by expansion projects, technological innovations, environmental initiatives, and ongoing geopolitical significance. These factors will ensure that the canal remains a linchpin of global trade, but they will also present new complexities that must be navigated carefully.

One of the most prominent aspects of the future of the Suez Canal is its continued expansion to accommodate the growing size of ships. Modern shipping vessels are becoming larger and more advanced, with supertankers, mega-container ships, and liquefied natural gas (LNG) carriers often dwarfing their predecessors. This trend is driven by the desire for greater efficiency in global trade, as larger ships can carry more cargo and reduce the cost per unit. However, the canal's original dimensions were not designed to accommodate vessels of this magnitude. The Suez Canal Authority (SCA) has already undertaken several expansion projects in recent years, most notably the creation of the New Suez Canal in 2015, which added a parallel waterway and increased the canal's capacity. Yet, further expansions will likely be necessary in the coming decades to ensure that the canal can handle the continued growth in ship size. This could involve deepening and widening sections of the canal, as well as upgrading the infrastructure that supports ship traffic, such as the canal's control systems and navigational aids.

The rise of automation and autonomous shipping is another major factor that will shape the future of the Suez Canal. As technology advances, the global shipping industry is increasingly looking towards automation to enhance efficiency, safety, and cost-effectiveness. Autonomous ships, which are capable of navigating without human intervention, are currently being developed and tested by major shipping companies. While fully autonomous vessels are not yet commonplace, their eventual widespread adoption could revolutionize the way ships travel through the Suez Canal. The canal will need to be equipped with the necessary digital infrastructure to accommodate these autonomous vessels, ensuring that they can safely navigate the waterway without human pilots. This could involve the installation of smart buoys, automated control systems, and real-time communication networks that allow autonomous ships to interact with the canal's control centers. Additionally, the SCA will need to work closely with international maritime organizations to develop new regulations and standards for the safe operation of autonomous ships in the canal.

Digitalization, more broadly, is expected to play a significant role in the future of the Suez Canal. As global trade becomes increasingly complex and interconnected, the need for real-time data and digital transparency will only grow. The Suez Canal will likely continue to embrace advanced digital tools such as big data analytics, artificial intelligence (AI), and machine learning to optimize its operations. These technologies can help the canal's authorities analyze vast amounts of data generated by ship traffic, environmental conditions, and global shipping trends, enabling more informed decision-making. AI systems could be used to predict potential bottlenecks or disruptions in the canal, while big data analytics can provide insights into how to improve the efficiency of convoys and reduce waiting times for ships. By leveraging these digital tools, the Suez Canal can maintain its status as one of the world's most efficient and reliable trade routes, even as the demands of global commerce continue to evolve.

Environmental sustainability will also be a critical consideration for the future of the Suez Canal. As concerns about climate change and environmental degradation grow, the canal must find ways to balance its role as a key trade route with its responsibility to protect the surrounding ecosystems. The Suez Canal passes through ecologically sensitive areas, including the Mediterranean and Red Seas, which are home to diverse marine life. The movement of ships through the canal can have a significant environmental impact, including the spread of invasive species through ballast water, pollution from ship emissions, and the potential for oil spills. In response to these challenges, the SCA is likely to implement stricter environmental regulations and adopt greener technologies to reduce the canal's ecological footprint. This could include requiring ships to use cleaner fuels, such as liquefied natural gas (LNG) or hydrogen, as well as adopting ballast water management systems to prevent the spread of invasive species. Additionally, the SCA could explore the use of renewable energy sources, such as solar and wind power, to reduce the canal's reliance on fossil fuels.

One of the most pressing environmental concerns for the future of the Suez Canal is the issue of rising sea levels. As global temperatures continue to increase, sea levels are expected to rise, which could have significant implications for the canal. Higher sea levels could affect the water depth in the canal, potentially altering the navigability of the waterway and necessitating further modifications to the canal's infrastructure. The SCA may need to invest in new technologies to monitor and manage the impact of rising sea levels, such as advanced water level sensors and real-time tide monitoring systems. Additionally, the SCA could work with international climate organizations to develop strategies for mitigating the long-term effects of climate change on the canal's operations.

Geopolitical dynamics will continue to influence the future of the Suez Canal as well. The canal has long been a focal point of international politics, given its strategic location and its importance to global trade. Control of the canal has historically been a source of tension between Egypt and other nations, and it remains a critical asset in Egypt's foreign policy. In the future, the Suez Canal is likely to remain a key geopolitical asset, especially as global trade shifts toward Asia and the Middle East. The canal's proximity to important energy-producing regions, such as the Persian Gulf, makes it a vital route for the transportation of oil and gas. As global energy markets continue to evolve, the Suez Canal will play a crucial role in the movement of energy resources, and its control will remain a priority for regional powers.

At the same time, the canal's geopolitical significance could expose it to new security challenges. As global trade becomes increasingly interconnected, the potential for disruptions to the canal's operations, whether through piracy, terrorism, or cyberattacks, will remain a concern. In response to these threats, the SCA will likely invest in advanced security measures to protect the canal and ensure the safety of the ships passing through it. This could include the deployment of surveillance drones, advanced radar systems, and cybersecurity infrastructure to guard against digital threats. Additionally, the canal's authorities may work closely with international naval forces to ensure that the canal remains secure from piracy and other maritime threats.

The future of the Suez Canal will also be shaped by broader shifts in global trade patterns. As emerging markets in Asia and Africa continue to grow, the demand for shipping routes that connect these regions to Europe and North America will increase. The Suez Canal is ideally positioned to facilitate this trade, and its importance as a global trade route is likely to grow in the coming decades. However, the canal will face competition from alternative routes, such as the Northern Sea Route, which is becoming more navigable due to melting Arctic ice.

To remain competitive, the SCA will need to continue investing in the canal's infrastructure and ensuring that it remains the fastest and most cost-effective option for shipping companies.

In the future, the Suez Canal could also play a role in the development of new shipping technologies, such as the use of hydrogen-powered vessels or ships that run on renewable energy. As the global shipping industry moves towards decarbonization, the canal could serve as a testing ground for these new technologies, helping to drive innovation in the maritime sector. By positioning itself at the forefront of green shipping technologies, the Suez Canal could become a leader in the global effort to reduce the environmental impact of international trade.

Another factor that will shape the future of the Suez Canal is the growth of digital trade and e-commerce. As more goods are bought and sold online, the demand for efficient shipping routes will continue to rise. The canal will need to adapt to the changing needs of e-commerce companies, which often require faster and more flexible shipping options. This could involve the development of new logistics hubs and infrastructure along the canal, allowing for quicker transshipment of goods. Additionally, the canal's authorities may explore partnerships with major e-commerce platforms to streamline the movement of goods through the waterway.

In conclusion, the future of the Suez Canal is likely to be marked by continued expansion, technological innovation, environmental responsibility, and geopolitical significance. As global trade continues to evolve, the canal will need to adapt to the growing size of ships, the rise of automation, and the increasing demand for digital transparency. At the same time, the canal must balance its role as a key trade route with its responsibility to protect the environment and address the challenges posed by climate change. Geopolitical dynamics will continue to influence the canal's operations, as it remains a vital asset in global energy markets and a focal point of international politics.

With ongoing investments in digital infrastructure, environmental sustainability, and security, the Suez Canal is well-positioned to remain one of the world's most important maritime routes for decades to come.

Epilogue

As we reach the end of our journey through the Suez Canal, it's clear that this waterway is much more than a simple passage for ships. It's a living link between continents, cultures, and histories—a testament to human ingenuity and our ability to shape the world around us.

From its ancient roots as a dream of connecting two seas to its role in modern global trade, the Suez Canal has been at the heart of countless stories that have shaped our world. We've explored how this remarkable channel was built, how it has influenced wars and politics, and how it continues to play a vital role in our global economy.

But the story of the Suez Canal is far from over. As the world continues to change, so too will the challenges and opportunities faced by this waterway. Environmental concerns, technological advancements, and global trade shifts will all play a part in its future.

As you close this book, remember that the Suez Canal is more than just a line on a map—it's a symbol of connection and collaboration. The next time you hear about a ship passing through the canal or see it on the news, you'll know the rich history and the incredible stories that have made the Suez Canal what it is today.

Thank you for taking this journey with us. Keep exploring, stay curious, and who knows—maybe one day, you'll be part of the next chapter in the history of the Suez Canal!

The End.